Window on the Chesapeake

This book is published in association with
and is funded in part by the

CHESAPEAKE   BAY

GATEWAYS   NETWORK

and the

U.S.   NATIONAL   PARK   SERVICE

To Mom and Dad,
who gave me the water and showed me the way.

— WMC

Beverly McMillan developed and edited this volume for the Mariners' Museum. Special appreciation goes to the following individuals at The Mariners' Museum: Publications: Betty Zattiero; Department of Photographic Services and Licensing: John Pemberton, Jason Copes, Claudia Jew, Anita Smith.

DESIGN: Kelly O'Neill, KSO Design ▪ Hampton, VA

COPYEDITING: Jon and Tam Kellogg

Library of Congress Cataloging-in-Publication Data

Clarke, Wendy Mitman, 1962-
    Window on the Chesapeake : the bay, its people and places / Wendy Mitman Clarke; photography by John Pemberton.
    p. cm.
    ISBN 0-917376-54-4 (pbk.)
    1. Chesapeake Bay Region (Md. and Va.)—Description and travel. 2. Chesapeake Bay Region (Md. and Va.)—Biography. 3. Chesapeake Bay Region (Md. and Va.)—Pictorial works. I. Pemberton, John, 1939- II. Title.

F187.C5 C58 2003
975.5'18—dc21

2002026446

11 10 09 08 07 06 05 04 03 02
10 9 8 7 6 5 4 3 2 1

Window on the Chesapeake

THE BAY, ITS PEOPLE AND PLACES

WENDY MITMAN CLARKE

THE MARINERS' MUSEUM
Newport News, Virginia

HOWELL PRESS
Charlottesville, Virginia

CONTENTS

New Point Comfort lighthouse, Mathews, VA

The Chesapeake Bay's physical parameters are easy enough to set down: The Bay's main stem is nearly 200 miles long, and while its deepest channel plunges 175 feet, on average the Bay is only twenty-seven feet deep. In its shimmering waters, Atlantic tides mingle with more than 150 tributaries draining portions of five states, from New York to Virginia. But the story—or, more accurately, the stories—of the Bay are far more complex than numbers alone can convey.

Always a highway for moving people and goods, the Bay and its environs have been a source of sustenance and raw materials for countless generations. In a steady cadence along its shores, people established settlements, towns and cities, experienced triumphs and tragedies, built economic enterprises, created rich cultural traditions and, for more than four centuries, helped shape the course of a nation. Throughout, the Bay has been explored, sampled, and otherwise scrutinized, yet these efforts at human understanding have advanced against an enduring background of mystery and wonder. The Chesapeake Bay is a place where the threads of water, nature, people and history interweave profoundly. It is this uniquely varied tapestry that the following pages attempt to capture, in the stories of an endangered lighthouse, lovely old boats, Bay artists and naturalists, watermen and conservationists—among others.

In 1998 Congress authorized the National Park Service to launch the Chesapeake Bay Gateways Network—a system uniting more than 100 independently operated parks, wildlife refuges, museums, historic communities and water trails in the Bay watershed. The Network's broad purpose is to deepen public appreciation of Bay stories and places, and to foster stewardship, conservation and restoration of the Bay and its watershed. Each a treasure in its own right, Network sites together tell the larger story of how water, place, nature and people are interconnected in the Chesapeake Bay region. Some of the profile subjects in this volume are Gateways, while others relate to Network sites described in sidebars. An appendix lists these Gateways and provides contact information readers can use to learn more about them.

This volume is graced by the vibrant writing of Wendy Mitman Clarke, executive editor of *Chesapeake Bay Magazine*. Much of the book's memorable photography is the work of Mariners' Museum photographer John Pemberton. Equally important to recognize is the generosity of the people whose stories follow, who shared their passion for the Bay and made this book possible.

John B. Hightower
President and CEO
The Mariners' Museum

Fran P. Mainella
Director
National Park Service

ONE STREAM AT A TIME

In the hilly farm country near Ephrata, Pennsylvania, God lives close to the red-tinted earth. You can see it in the hand-written signs quoting scripture in front of tidy brick homes—one phrase per side, so you get a little religion coming and going. You can see it on the storefronts, posted with the note "Closed for Ascension Day." It's in the bowed heads of Amish women who kneel in riotously blooming flower beds, and in the stoic shoulders of men as they guide teams of mules at the plow. From here, the watermen and oysters and long, flat horizons of the Chesapeake Bay seem a world away, as distant as the moon. And that, in a nutshell, is the problem.

Matt Ehrhart steers his pickup along narrow roads flanked with daisies and honeysuckle, slowing down every time he crosses a stream. He's meandering along Indian Run, a creek like hundreds of others in this neck of southern Pennsylvania—that is to say shallow, narrow, fairly slow, and profoundly important to the Bay some thirty miles distant. "This is where it starts to go downhill, right here," he says, as he pulls over across from a barn perched atop a low hill. There is no grass on the hillside, just an acre or so of pocked brown ooze—courtesy of the cows that walk from the barnyard down to the skinny creek at the bottom, where they drink, swat flies, defecate, chew cud and generally hang out. Across the street, more cows are doing the same in a narrow stretch of pasture along the stream. "See, almost that whole area should be a buffer," Matt says, shaking his head. "We are still working on this guy."

Several miles away, he pulls over again and points to a grassy swath embracing both sides of the same creek. The grass is thick and lush, and saplings and low shrubs stretch skyward. The cows here are still doing their bovine thing, but well away from the creek. "When we first sampled this stream we were just sampling manure, half-digested silage," Matt says. "Just a year later there was a real bottom and actually critters crawling around in it. To watch [the buffer] come in and start looking like a forest is pretty satisfying, really."

As assistant director and watershed restoration manager for the Chesapeake Bay Foundation's Pennsylvania office in Harrisburg, thirty-three-year-old Matt finds in untarnished streams the kind of glory and gratification an opera buff might find in a Puccini aria. He has been seduced by them since he was a boy growing up in nearby New Holland. He has flailed away at them with a fly rod, he has watched his young son find the same wondrous world within their riffles and pools. He has made his home on one here near Ephrata, a sun-dappled, silver ribbon called Segloch Run, one of a handful of streams in southern Pennsylvania healthy enough to support a population of wild trout. He wants to make every creek and brook within this place of red earth, green hills and devout people look, sound and feel like this one.

It is a vital goal for the Chesapeake Bay, because nearly half of its watershed—almost 30,000 square miles—is in Pennsylvania. The top sources of nitrogen in the Bay are cropland, point sources (like sewage treatment plants), urban and other agricultural runoff—and Pennsylvania contributes 40 percent of that, the vast majority in its cropland. Among all the river basins that feed the Bay, the Susquehanna River basin is the top contributor, carrying 44 percent of the Bay's nitrogen (the Potomac River basin is a distant second at 22 percent). In terms of phosphorus, Pennsylvania ranks third at 18 percent, with cropland again being the major culprit. Pennsylvania's Conestoga River alone—of which Indian Run is a tributary—dumps more sediment and nutrients into the Bay than any other tributary in the entire Bay watershed, Matt says. Scientists state it in percentages, but the old saying of you-know-what rolling downhill can be taken quite literally when it comes to Pennsylvania and its relationship to the Bay.

So how to stop it? One way is to repair the state's streams and wetlands so they're better able to filter it out before it ever heads south. "The whole thing started about five or six years ago when the Chesapeake Bay Foundation realized that just stopping existing pollution wasn't enough, that we needed to start restoring critical parts of the ecosystem," Matt says. "On the Bay, that means oyster beds and submerged aquatic vegetation. Up here, that means riparian and forest buffers." According to the foundation, studies within the watershed have found that one acre of buffer can remove one ton of sediment a year, twenty-eight pounds of nitrogen and two-and-one-half pounds of phosphorus. A Pennsylvania Fish and Boat Commission study of a creek near Intercourse, Pennsylvania, found that as the streamside regained its green borders, the creek narrowed by about a third, gained speed and re-established a gravel bottom, which fish need for successful spawning. The number of fish in the creek nearly doubled, as did the number of small invertebrates.

When Matt, who has a master's degree in engineering science and hydrology, first signed on with Chesapeake Bay Foundation (CBF) as its Pennsylvania watershed restoration specialist, the CBF was focused on grass-roots programs—volunteer tree plantings and the like. Matt agrees that such things are necessary and helpful, but they make the scientist in him squirm a little. He knew that if the organization was really going to make a difference in stream restoration, it would have to do it on a wholesale, professional level. And he knew that to sell it to the farmers he'd grown up around, it would have to benefit *them*, not just some oyster reef in the Bay. "People up here think big water is Raystown Lake. We need to say, 'Do this for your neighbor, your kids, your farm, your stream.'"

Working in tandem with similar state and federal programs, CBF helps farmers buffer their streams and wetlands at little or no cost. The most basic project is to first build a stabilized crossing through a creek, then fence off the buffer area around it and plant native shrubs and trees. The farmer pays for the crossing; the foundation pays for the rest. But that's just a start. Under CBF's program, the minimum buffer width is fifteen feet, and if the farmer fences off more, he earns "best management practices" credits that are given a dollar value he can apply to other projects on the farm. For instance, if he widens the buffer he can often earn enough credits to pay for his cost of building the crossing. In Berks County, for example, a farmer fenced ten acres of wetlands and wider stream buffers that earned him $10,000 worth of credits. He used them to pay for his portion of a barnyard run-off control project that helped keep manure out of a nearby stream. Matt also sells the idea based on pure economics—cows standing around in muddy swales and creeks are far more prone to illnesses like mastitis, which cost the farmer in vet bills and poor milk production. Cleaner drinking water is also a benefit, and once the buffer is fenced off, it's easy for the farmer to create smaller fenced paddocks and promote rotational grazing. "The first thing we hear is, 'I have lower vet bills and happier, healthier cows,' " Matt says. "The second thing we hear is, 'For the first time since Grandpa had the farm the kids can fish in the stream, we can picnic by the stream.'"

By early 2002, the foundation had eight subcontracted employees selling and delivering the work, with projects lined up out the door. The program had fenced 500 miles of buffer and about 1,800 acres of wetlands, Matt says. The foundation estimates there are up to 4,000 miles left to do. "When we started all this and people had done five miles, the number five hundred seemed completely unrealistic. We've probably done four hundred of those five hundred miles in the last two years, so maybe four thousand miles is not so unrealistic."

After buffer-building comes research—learning what, exactly, they are accomplishing. "What happens after you build the fence and plant the trees, we just don't know a lot about," Matt says. "What kind of recovery takes place and how long it takes for different species." Using the pristine Segloch Run as a baseline, Matt and his staff take samples of the stream bottom and water—thirty-two samples of one square foot each—and examine everything they find there, animal, chemical, mineral. They do the same in Indian Run. What they're finding so far is that the restored streams quickly flush out sediment and regain their gravel bottoms. The banks stop eroding, water flow improves and the bugs and insects needed to support fish life return. So do fish, as well as the smaller critters like crayfish. Two to three years after the creek's channels are re-established, Matt says, the trees are starting to develop canopies and the creekside is alive with flowers and shrubs and insects. "That's when you smile and say, barring some disaster, this one is coming back."

Some six years into the program, Matt and his staff are wrestling with all that still needs to be done. They're studying how to make the buffers even more cost-effective, how to lower farmers' costs, what flora grows best—and of course all the minutiae that entails, such as what kind of trunk tubes best protect the saplings from deer and rodents. The stream research is ongoing. And CBF is now looking for ways to get residential property owners into the program. For the boy who grew up seduced by Pennsylvania's streams, the affair has only just begun. ■

Susquehanna Water Trails

As the Chesapeake Bay's largest tributary, the scenic Susquehanna River is an alluring highway for getting to know some of the loveliest country in the northern Bay region. Canoeists, kayakers, and boaters have a wealth of choices for day trips or overnights exploring the Susquehanna's beauty, punctuated with chances for excursions to riverside communities. A series of five water trails exist or are under development, including stretches along the river's main stem, its west branch and two tributaries. The Susquehanna River Trail was the first water trail in the Bay watershed. It begins in Sunbury, Pennsylvania and traverses fifty lush miles to Harrisburg. Different sites along its length provide primitive camping facilities on river islands or convenient bases for day paddles.

Among the other water trails under development is the Lower Susquehanna Water Trail, which begins in Harrisburg and will extend another sixty-five miles to the Susquehanna's confluence with the Chesapeake Bay near Havre de Grace, Maryland.

CARVER'S SONG

Wick, wick, wick. The sound of the drawknife against soft cedar is gentle and smooth, as peels of wood curl off and flutter to the dusty floor and the head of a canvasback slowly takes shape. The rough-hewn hands of sixty-eight-year-old James "Jimmy" Pierce will carve a few dozen delicate heads of the gorgeous Bay waterfowl, the shavings drifting around his feet like sweet-smelling snow, before he sands them down and then takes a much smaller knife and whittles in the details, the curve of the cheek just so, the bridge of the beak a sharp, reversed V. He has been doing this, over and over, for fifty-three years and he never tires of it. Maybe that's because with each pull of the knife over the wood he knows he is paying a sort of tribute. The wick, wick, wick is like the quiet background music in his home of Havre de Grace, Maryland, a place where the carving of decoys runs as deep and long as the mighty Susquehanna River beside it.

Jimmy grew up here. "All I had to do was climb over the fence and I was on the river," he says. "I've hunted and fished all my life." When he was younger, the watermen would trap-net for perch in the spring and pound-net out on the Susquehanna Flats for shad and herring, then haul seine for rockfish in the summer. Come autumn, it would be time to head out on the river to gun for geese and ducks—and so a man would need some decoys to lure the waterfowl close. "Everybody who was a waterman was a boatbuilder and a decoy carver," he says. "If you wanted a boat, you built it yourself; and if you wanted to hunt, you made decoys."

The birds were, in other words, made for a working purpose. They were tools. And Jimmy remains true to that: nearly all of his birds are life-size, all made with a lead or wooden keel under the belly and a ring to tie it to the rest of the rig—a hunter's name for the flock of decoys he uses to entice waterfowl within shooting range. The birds are artful but simple, elegant yet durable. "Even the decoys I make for collectors, they could throw 'em overboard and shoot over 'em," he says. It's not that he dislikes the highly refined, decorative decoys that have become a fine art form. But what he makes represents something else, something far more important to him. The labor and art of carving working decoys is in his hands and his heart—it is who he is. "Years ago, it was a way of life, and it was a way to put food on the table to eat," he says. "The best in a working decoy is probably one that's been worked for fifty years. It's got shot in it, the head's been replaced four times, it's got cracks in it. That's *history* there. The one that sat on a mantle all those years never saw the water."

To listen to Jimmy is to learn about a lot more than decoys. Leaning back in a dusty chair, his ample belly comfortably front and center, he punctuates most sentences with, "You know what I'm sayin'?" as he reveals himself to be as much philosopher as carver, ruminating freely on topics from sedimentation in the Susquehanna watershed to what defines "art." Through it all, history and tradition trickle like a steady stream.

Beside him, a chocolate Labrador named Casey lies quietly on the floor, happily gnawing a chunk of wood into splinters. The shop where Jimmy and his thirty-three-year-old son Charlie work together, annually turning out about 800 decoys representing some forty species, is as comfortable and purposeful as a pair of well-worn hip waders. Wood dust dominates the decor. It drifts in corners and beneath sanders, it sifts like fine flour from the hanging fluorescent lights. Things are slightly less dusty upstairs, where a few mounted racks of deer antlers loom over a long workbench covered in tools, and patterns of the heads of hen mallards and mergansers, bluebills and buffleheads hang from the rafters. Back in the paint room, shelves are stacked top to bottom with decoys in various stages of painting. On a low table in the room's center, silver cans of paint congregate, and small rafts of brushes, each for a specific task, are stacked here and there. Paint is spattered everywhere, and on the one clean wall by the phone, names, numbers and even a few orders are scribbled in pencil wherever the scribbler could squeeze in the room. Dusty posters for various decoy shows and waterfowl festivals are tacked up here and there, and in one corner a framed watercolor shows a bunch of deer whooping it up at a backwoods camp, the hunters hanging upside down, toe tags dangling.

Jimmy was just fourteen when he began working part-time at the shop of the late R. Madison Mitchell, Havre de Grace's undertaker and also its most renowned decoy maker. The town was full of notable carvers, but Mitchell was the undisputed dean. He knew how to carve birds that attracted waterfowl, that could ride any weather, and that were elegant and beautiful. He also knew how to make a lot of them—after all, hunters needed dozens of birds to fill out their rigs, not one or two. Mitchell turned out something like 100,000 decoys in his working lifetime, and more importantly, he gave freely of his talent and skills, passing his knowledge along to apprentices and youngsters who would carry the tradition forward. One of them was Jimmy Pierce.

Even while he worked full-time as a cable splicer for Bell Telephone, Jimmy always worked on birds, whittling heads during his spare time or when he was on the road. In 1989 he retired from Bell Telephone and started making decoys full-time, eventually teaching his son, Charlie, the craft as well. (Full-time is relative, of course: "There's only twelve months in a year and we play for two months. After Christmas my son and I go hunting for three or four weeks, maybe whittle some heads. And now it's spring and we want to go fishing.")

To this day, the Pierces use the same methods Jimmy learned in R. Madison Mitchell's shop. The birds begin out back as piles of half-sawn tree trunks that are cut to manageable blocks on a well-used thirty-six-inch band saw. (Jimmy uses white pine or polonia for the birds' bodies, basswood or cedar for their heads.) From there, the chunks of wood are attached to a reciprocating lathe—a machine that uses a rough template, called a pattern, of the bird's body to cut a matching form out of the shapeless block. From there, Jimmy sands the rough bodies on a belt sander, then "breasts and tails" them—shapes the breast and tail on a drum sander. The bodies are examined for any imperfections—cracks or knots in the wood—and patched if need be.

Jimmy makes the head in a similar way, roughing the shape out first, then slowly refining it using a router, sander, drawknife and spoke shave—a purpose-built tool that has a small curved blade wedged firmly in the center of a spindle of wood. The delicate work of whittling the face and, if it's a collector's bird, perhaps some of the feathers, is done last. He attaches the heads to the bodies with epoxy, then does a final sanding before painting them. Jimmy paints in oils and uses a technique Mitchell developed called wet-on-wet—applying wet coats on top of one another to create a graceful, feathery result.

Jimmy reckons it would take about eight hours to make a bird by itself, start to finish, but that's not how he learned and it's not how he has taught Charlie. They will make dozens of a certain type at a time, finishing each stage of the process for each group of birds before moving on to the next.

Decoy carver at work at Havre de Grace Decoy Museum

Havre de Grace Decoy Museum

Jimmy Pierce's love of history goes beyond his work carving decoys—he's also on the governing board of the Havre de Grace Decoy Museum, and it's not unusual to find him there. Located along the Susquehanna River at the southern end of town, the museum is dedicated to decoys and the hunting and gunning traditions from which they emanated. More than 1,200 decoys are on display here, as well as exhibits that explain the evolution of waterfowling and decoy carving through generations. Set in a marsh-like surrounding, the waterfowling exhibit includes various boats used by local hunters through the years (sneakboxes, sink-boxes and punt gun skiffs) as well as their weaponry—muzzleloaders and shotguns dating from the 1800s.

R. Madison Mitchell is remembered here in two major displays, one of which includes a recording of him describing the community of carvers in Havre de Grace in the 1930s, '40s and '50s. Upstairs in a long, bright room with floor-to-ceiling windows facing the water, about a dozen carvers are profiled and their work exhibited, Jimmy among them. "The best part of the museum," Jimmy says, "is that we honored a lot of these people before they died, and a hundred years from now, it's all going to be there."

"This is the same way they've been doing it for a hundred years," he says. "They were doing it for hunters who needed two dozen birds. It's the same process for miniatures or a full-size bird."

Jimmy's decoys go to collectors all over the world, and his is a refreshingly simple system: "I'll mail a bird and if you don't like 'im, don't keep 'im. If you do, send me a check." Meeting people, "from multimillionaires to people who don't have nothing, know what I'm sayin'?" has been one of the unexpected perks of this career. So has been the chance to teach his son all he has learned, and to work and hunt side by side with him. But fundamentally, it's the love of the craft and all that it represents that brings him into the dusty shop nearly every day, where the wick, wick, wick of a drawknife will murmur and resonate for as long as Jimmy Pierce has two good hands to pull it. And even when this is no longer possible, that soft, steady music will play on. ■

Window on the Chesapeake

KEEPING THE SHIPS MOVING

"Delicate" isn't a word one would associate with a sixty-foot, 800hp tugboat pushing a barge loaded with 1,330 tons of diesel oil. Nevertheless, delicate is *Mitzie Hughes* when her captain, Mark McCluskey, sidles her up to the 866-foot cruise ship *Galaxy*, which has just docked at Dundalk Marine Terminal in Baltimore. "You up there, Tom?" Mark asks engineer Tom Patzold, 200 feet away on the bow of the pragmatically named *DS13* (DS for double-skinned), the bunker barge *Mitzie* is pushing today. "Yeah," Tom answers, talking into a remote radio dangling from his sweatshirt.

"Where's this bunker connection? Up forward?"

"Yeah." Up forward, it turns out, right behind a bus-sized door in the towering side of the blue-and-white cruise ship that says, in no uncertain terms, "No Tug." If Mark so much as taps that door with *DS13* he could crush it, dent it or otherwise ruin his day. Yet he has to place the bow of the barge just forward of it so his deck crew can tie off to a huge cleat recessed into the ship's side. Then they can do what they came here for on this blustery summer morning—pump 8,700 barrels, or about 352,000 gallons, of No. 6 diesel into the ship's tanks. "Okay, about three more feet here," Tom's voice crackles from the radio. Mark begins a complex dance of throttle, clutch and rudder to maneuver the barge into just the right place. "This is kind of like a bull in a china shop," he says. "You've got to be careful where you touch it." Steve Winwood is quietly singing "Roll With It Baby" on a portable radio in the tug's wheelhouse, and just as *DS13* is about to touch the ship's side the wheelhouse telephone rings, as does Mark's pager. "Wouldn't you know it," he grumbles. He ignores them, never taking his eyes or hands from the dicey job before him.

"Couple feet," Tom says. The tug's twin 400 hp Detroit Diesels two decks below the wheelhouse rumble and roar as Mark works the throttles, and her two massive propellers churn and rip the dark water. But in a minute or two, it's done—the bow of *DS13* just kisses the side of the *Galaxy* right where it's supposed to, deckhand Ross Gaither slips a line over the cleat, and in another moment, the barge and tug are snug against the ship's side. On the barge, tankerman Andrew Bendis leaps to action, maneuvering a white gantry crane from which a six-inch fuel line dangles like an elephant's trunk. He'll snake this hose into yet another door in the side of the ship, where the ship's engineers will bolt it to an enormous manifold. Four hours or so of pumping at about 88,000 gallons per hour, and *Galaxy* will be ready to leave, her fuel bunkers topped off, her decks full of daiquiri-sipping passengers, bound for waters far bluer than those in the hard-working shoulders of Baltimore's harbor.

Galaxy belongs to Celebrity Cruises, which came to Baltimore in spring 2002 amid great fanfare. Snaring the lucrative cruise ship business was a feather in the Port of Baltimore's cap, yet another sign of the port's diversification and growth. And it's no surprise that *Mitzie Hughes* and *DS13* are the

regular fuel pumps for the port's glamorous new customer. Both are
workhorses for Vane Brothers Company, which opened for business as a ship
chandlery in 1898 in the city's Fells Point district. Like the port, Vane Brothers
endured the tectonic shift from sail to steam, from graceful schooners delivering watermelons and timber to gigantic, boxy car carriers unloading
thousands of Toyotas, and container ships stacked with Nikes and Sony TVs.
The company has seen the port at its grittiest, when raucous, hustling wharves
lined Light and Pratt streets and rough-and-tumble shipyards perched along
Key Highway. Today, Light and Pratt streets are the centerpiece of the Inner
Harbor's renaissance, driven by millions of tourists who visit the National
Aquarium, the Maryland Science Center and the dozens of stores and restaurants that hug the waterfront. Fells Point overflows with hip young things and
trendy bars and shops to serve them. Key Highway is home to one of the
harbor's snazziest marinas, high-rise condo complexes and a couple of waterfront restaurants. The rough-edged, industrial business of running a thriving
port has been moved to the harbor's outer edges, but thrive the port still does.

Like the port, Vane Brothers has evolved—grindingly at times, fluidly at
others—and the company digs deep into the rich loam of its history to
remind it of where it has been and where it has to yet go. Throughout, Vane
Brothers has provided the stuff that keeps the ships moving. In the age of
sail, that included blocks, rope, foul-weather gear, blackstrap molasses,
salted eggs, fatback and cod. Today it's oil, millions of barrels a year moving
from Maine to the Carolinas and bunkering (fueling) ships, power plants,
even navy destroyers.

"We have changed a lot," says C. Duff Hughes, the company's enthusiastic,
boyish forty-four-year-old president, whose grandfather, Charles F. Hughes

Sr., partnered with the Vanes in 1920. "We really are aware of the need to change when the environment calls for it. Right now we're dealing with OPA 90 [the Oil Pollution Act of 1990] and reskinning the fleet [building double-hulled barges, like *DS13*]. That's one focus. And the other is to expand when there's an opportunity. We've never been bashful about jumping into something that looks like a good opportunity."

Vane Brothers opened in 1898 when schooner captains William Burke Vane and his brother Allen, both from Maryland's Eastern Shore, decided to hang up their sea boots and use their hard-earned knowledge to build a business catering to shipping needs. The Hughes family got involved in 1919, when a distant Vane cousin and schooner captain, Claude Hughes, joined the business. (He was in love, and his bride-to-be wanted him off the water.) A year later he brought along his brother, Charles F. Hughes Sr., and the two quickly became an indispensible element of the partnership. With the Vanes, they built a shipbuilding company that owned dozens of schooners and a chandlery that provided critical supplies and services for East Coast seamen. In her book *Time and the Tide*, Mary Butler Davies quotes D'arcy Grant, a journalist from Philadelphia who left her desk to become captain of the schooner *Fannie Insley*. "Vane's is the one spot on the Eastern seaboard where you can look forward with any hope of certainty to meeting a sailing man you want to see," D'arcy wryly wrote in a *Baltimore Sun* article in June 1940. "If you sit beside the stove in Vane's long enough everything on two legs that sails a Bay freighter will come in through the door... It is a comfort to know that whatever happens to any of us out there, the Hughes boys, Claude and Charley, and Captain Vane are standing by."

By World War II, the Hughes owned the business outright. Allen Vane had died in 1941, and Captain William Burke Vane, who had never quite swallowed the bitter pill of the sailing ships' demise, sold out his remaining shares. The Hughes brothers took advantage of the times. With a small tanker called *Hughes Bros*, they supplied galley fuel to Liberty ships and provisioned Coast Guard vessels. By the late 1940s, as the beautiful old schooners died in the backwaters of Curtis Bay, the harbor filled with tugs, tankers and freighters. The chandlery continued—moving, over the years, from Fells Point to Pratt Street and then back to Fells Point—but supplying diesel to the new fleet of ships and tugs was rapidly dominating the company's business. In 1951, Charles Hughes Jr., Duff's father, joined the firm, as Claude retired.

By the 1970s, Vane Brothers was back in the ship-owning business, commissioning smallish motor tankers that would cement

Seven Foot Knoll lighthouse

Seven Foot Knoll Lighthouse

For 133 years, the entrance to Baltimore's harbor was marked by the picturesque Seven Foot Knoll lighthouse. The oldest screwpile-design lighthouse in Maryland, the light had a fourth-order Fresnel lens that could be seen for twelve miles. Automated after World War II, the light was decommissioned as an active Bay navigation aid in the 1980s. In 1988 it was moved by barge and crane to the Inner Harbor, where it stands today. Now restored, the Seven Foot Knoll light is located on Pier 5 and is part of the Baltimore Maritime Museum, which also features the lightship *Chesapeake* that marked entry to the Chesapeake Bay for many years.

the company's commitment to the niche of bunkering ships. When Duff joined the company in 1980 after graduating from Denison University, the chandlery was still operating (it finally closed in 1994), but Duff saw opportunity in providing other critical fluids to ships: marine lubricants, water and both No. 2 diesel (marine-grade diesel fuel) and No. 6 diesel (a thicker, heavier fluid that ships mix with No. 2). Several small companies in Baltimore divvied up these services; Duff orchestrated their consolidation under the Vane Brothers flag. He also earned his tankerman's ticket and his master's license and worked on the water to get the new enterprise going. It provided him with hands-on knowledge of exactly how things work in the port and what his crews would face day-in and day-out.

Today, Vane Brothers owns fifteen tugs, forty barges, two motor launches and two motor tankers. Its main base is on three piers in the harbor's Canton district (soon to move to a brand new facility in Fairfield, near Curtis Bay) and two satellite bases in Norfolk and Philadelphia. Tug and barge crews work 24/7 for two weeks, then have two weeks off. "It has taken us years to get the right crews who can work together for two weeks at a time," Duff says. "There's a lot of nepotism in the industry, but it works. We've found that when you need this in-the-wheelhouse experience, it's the fathers who can teach the sons this work."

After the 1989 *Exxon Valdez* accident in Alaska's Prince William Sound, Congress passed the Oil Pollution Act of 1990 (OPA 90) which requires barges like Vane's (5,000 gross tons and under) to be double-hulled by 2015. Under Duff's aggressive leadership, Vane Brothers is already well on its way to compliance, with four retired Coast Guardsmen on staff overseeing safety, training and inspection of the entire fleet, and new 365-foot, double-skinned barges under construction. It all seems a long way from the days when schooners ghosted down the rivers of the Eastern Shore, Baltimore-bound with watermelons and tomatoes, and seamen warmed their hands by the stove at Vane Brothers chandlery. But when Duff Hughes swings his two young sons onto *Mitzie Hughes* for a ride in Baltimore's Harbor, it's suddenly not very far at all. ■

DREAM BUILDER

Even sitting still, *Pride of Baltimore II* seems to fly. Her hull is lean as a greyhound, her spars thrown back like an ornery thoroughbred tossing its mane. In these days of generic plastic boats, she is the best kind of throwback, a reminder that beauty born of function is worthy in and of itself. Just to look at her makes something in our hearts' collective maritime past stir and murmur, and we long to feel the wet wild breath of the sea. There is a hopeless romance to her and all that she can do, while we are tied here, clod-footed, to the land. How can one beautiful ship evoke so much? Perhaps in part because the man who built her knows both lives well—the sea and the land—and understands the necessity and the lure of each.

On the face of it, C. Peter Boudreau lives an ordinary, contented suburban life in Annapolis, Maryland. His wife, Martha, commutes to the Washington, D.C., area every day to her job managing a public relations firm. His daughters—Louise, eight, and Madeleine, ten—attend school and giggle as girls will. But when Peter heads into his office and turns to his singular work, he will draw on his lifetime love of big sailing ships to help him create fleet and beautiful vessels that merge the romance and beauty of the past with the needs and requirements of contemporary ships. In the world of yacht and ship design, his is a niche as narrow as the tip of a marlinspike. And it's one for which he seemed destined.

While most of us grew up firmly stuck to land and the trappings of urban life, Peter and his four siblings lived in the Caribbean, where their father, Captain Walter Boudreau, ran a series of graceful charter schooners and their mother, Terry, operated a small hotel. In their remote lagoon on Marigot Bay in St. Lucia, Peter's parents helped launch what is today's thriving charter boat industry. Along with his brothers and sisters, Peter played in the island's barely tamed jungle and sailed big wooden ships. He was still in diapers when he made his first transatlantic passage on *Caribee*, coincidentally a replica of *Pride of Baltimore II*'s breed of Baltimore clipper. Peter became a regular hand on his father's ships, working aboard almost every summer from the time he was about eleven years old. "It was an interesting way to grow up," he says, though not all sparkling spray and dazzling days. The caprail on his father's ship *Janeen*, for example, was 110 feet long on each side. That's a lot of sandpaper and varnish. "You felt like you could go your whole life and never get there," he says. But he also learned the deep satisfaction and quiet thrill of being part of a crew making a big, complex ship sail in any weather. "I learned how streamlined that can get, you basically don't even talk. I like that when no one says a word, but things just happen flawlessly time after time." Peter emerged from the experience with an understanding and appreciation of ships and skills that most people had long forgotten or considered archaic. "It's almost like guidance he [his father] instilled in me, that there's value in these ships and traditions."

Pride of Baltimore II

Value, perhaps, but not a particularly stable life. By the time he left the Caribbean in the mid-1970s and started crewing and skippering a variety of "school" ships—vessels used in sail training programs like Outward Bound—he realized he was tiring of the vagrant life inherent to the sea. On a trip to Baltimore, he saw the first *Pride of Baltimore* taking shape along the harbor waterfront, and the path suddenly seemed clear. "I took whatever they would give me, which was shoveling wood chips. I never even thought about things like getting to and from work, buying groceries, getting a place to live, needing clothes! I had a pair of shorts, flip-flops and shades. It was an amazing experience. Actually building a boat was a brand new challenge. It was a learning thing for me, because I didn't have any real skills to bring to it, just brawn and a willingness to work hard. And we did work hard."

When *Pride* set sail, Peter had plenty of skills to bring to it, and he quickly became one of the ship's masters. But again, he found he did not love the captain's life quite as passionately as had his father. Eventually he returned to Baltimore, and was building the 104-foot pungy schooner *Lady Maryland* when the *Pride* sank in a squall off Puerto Rico on May 14, 1986, taking its captain and three crew. "*Pride I* was devastating to everybody," he says. But almost immediately, the foundation that operated the ship announced plans to build another. This time, Peter was the master builder. "In some ways, it would have been an affront for anyone else to build it," he says. Designed by Tom Gillmer, the ship has been a resounding success in its role as worldwide ambassador for Maryland, largely because the ship is beautiful and sails, as Peter says, like a witch—fast, strong, steady. "I love sailing that boat because she's remarkable in being able to get up to ten, eleven, twelve knots in almost nothing. It's the right combination of tonnage, sail area and hull shape."

A few years after finishing *Pride II*, Peter became a partner in Tri-Coastal Marine, a company that specializes in the design and construction of traditional ships and the preservation and restoration of historic ships. Among the firm's best-known credits are the Baltimore clipper *Amistad* (a replica of the slave ship *La Amistad*), *Spirit of Massachusetts*, and the unique conservation of the USS *Constellation*, launched in 1854 and the last sailing warship built by the Navy. The company has also designed the 120-foot, steel-hulled topsail schooner *Great Circle*, a sail-training vessel for the Ocean Classroom Foundation, as well as the *Spirit of Enterprize* for the National Maritime Heritage Foundation in Washington, D.C.

Boudreau believes more recreational sailors are looking at older, proven designs that sail brilliantly and seeing their beauty and their merit. "I think people are looking at traditional designs and hull shapes and saying, 'Hey, do we really need six feet of headroom?' Some of the older day-sailing designs are just so much fun to sail." Peter also wants to focus less on historic restorations and more on designing and building new boats for new uses, modifying generations-old designs to better accommodate the needs of the present. For instance, a venture called the Schooner Virginia Project calls for a reproduction of the type of schooner Virginia pilots once raced out to ships that were waiting to be guided into the Chesapeake. He and a colleague are modifying the design so the vessel will pass Coast Guard passenger requirements and make it easier for it to accomplish its mission, which is similar to that of *Pride of Baltimore II*.

Above all, what counts for Peter is a boat's ability to sail and its beauty. It should be lovely to set eyes upon, and it should sail like a banshee. So it's not surprising that his own thirty-six-foot wooden ketch *Alaria*, which he keeps in his neighborhood marina, was designed and built by L. Francis Herreshoff, one of the nation's most renowned designers, whose boats were known the world over for their beauty and sailability. "I absolutely love it. For me it's the perfect boat. She's just built beautifully." It's not unusual for Peter to pack up *Alaria* on a Friday evening and head out with his family, finding a nook of a creek for his daughters to dinghy around in, a place where he can hang the oil lamp from the boom and contemplate the peace of the water. There's seawater in his veins, no doubt, and he does miss the sailing life sometimes. But the Bay, in its myriad beauty, is beguiling enough in her own special way for the son of the schooner captain, this builder of beautiful, fleet sailing ships. ▪

Pride of Baltimore II

A replica of an 1812-era topsail schooner, the *Pride of Baltimore II* spends its days as an active sail-training vessel. In the winter months the 185-ton *Pride* berths at Locust Point in Baltimore Harbor, undergoing meticulous maintenance, from painting and varnishing to engine tune-ups. With the coming of spring the sleek ship departs for ports along the mid-Atlantic coast and beyond. Would-be "salts" who want to experience the romance and adventure of tall-ship sailing can book passage as guest crew members for trips ranging from two to ten days. Even a short visit to the *Pride II* provides a great opportunity to learn about the key role such swift schooners played as trade vessels in the Chesapeake Bay.

BAY SONGS AND BEER

Like a great, graceful white bird, the schooner *Woodwind* has flown across the Chesapeake Bay and back, and this evening she's sailing into the sun setting over the Statehouse dome in Annapolis when Jeff Holland takes the wheel and eases into his epic poem, *Blood of the Bold Picaroon*. Until now, the boat's cargo of tourists haven't been paying much attention to Jeff and his cohort Kevin Brooks, better known as the Annapolis-based singing-songwriting team of Them Eastport Oyster Boys. Perhaps the visitors can be forgiven; few sights are as distractingly lovely as Annapolis Harbor at sunset from the deck of a lively sailing ship. But as his voice slowly builds over the water, Jeff's rollicking story of the pirate named Captain Doubloon—a tale loosely based on pirate Richard Clarke's plan in 1707 to sack Annapolis and steal its arms and ammunition—pulls them in. "His veins

carried nothing but water and ice;/Yes, a cold-blooded creature he happened to be,/With no trace of mercy or charity;/He'd capture a ship, make the crew walk the plank,/And he'd never say, 'Please,' 'You're welcome,' or 'Thanks.' " By the time Jeff reaches the tale's bombastic climax, and the cabin boy Bonny Hugh has cleverly scuttled Doubloon's plan by burning his ship to the waterline with coals from the galley stove, there's no sound on *Woodwind* but the hiss of her bow wave, Kevin's quiet accompaniment on banjo, and Jeff, roaring and whispering and pretty much having a jolly time. Once the tale is over, Jeff exchanges the wheel for his baritone ukulele, the Oyster Boys break into a lively calypso song about a blustery day sailing on the Bay, and the crowd is hooked for the duration. "It's a lot of work because it's hard to grab people's attention," Jeff says of their weekly performances on *Woodwind*, one of the Oyster Boys' many gigs. "But it's really our creative time," Kevin says. "We go out for two hours, meet people from all over the world and show them why we love this place, that this is why we're here."

Why they love this place—the Bay broadly, and Annapolis's maritime heart, the neighborhood called Eastport, more specifically—has to do with the details. Worn-out boat shoes. Smelly wet dogs who shake all over you. Crabbing. A history richer than a pirate's buried treasure. Maryland beaten biscuits. A good sailors' pub. A lovely white workboat, lonely and old. The sight of the sun setting over the water. A fine breeze in the evening. All are grist for their songwriting mill, and as Jeff points out with unadorned awe in his voice, he can't get over how fertile the creative soil is. "It's a person or place or a thing you wouldn't find anywhere else, and it's a huge treasure trove of inspiration—anyone you talk to, anytime you go on a boat ride, anytime you see a beautiful view. There's just *so much.*"

Jeff came to Annapolis on a sailboat with his father in 1981 and never left. A playful wordsmith and history fanatic, he took a job directing public relations for the U.S. Boat Shows and, as always, kept writing songs and poetry and stories on the side. He took up the ukulele by accident—picked one up while house-sitting at a friend's. He had never considered himself a musician; guitars and their six strings always intimidated him. "I don't know about anyone else," he says, "but I only have four fingers. The uke has four strings. Four fingers. Okay." In the mid-1980s he teamed up with Janie Meneely and Chris Noyes to form the group Crab Alley. Their idea was to dig around in the Bay's musical closet and haul out all the old sea songs they just *knew* had to be part of the Bay's rich waterborne culture. But they couldn't find any. Only three could they directly attribute to the Bay; a turn-of-the-century steamboat song called "Sailing Down the Chesapeake Bay," an oysterman's lament called "The Shanghaied Drudger," and that old favorite, "The Star-Spangled Banner." It turns out that the Bay's watermen just weren't the types to belt out tunes as they tonged oysters and netted crabs (these days they tend to listen to the chatter on their VHF radios at high volume). "Rather than let the dearth of material stop us, we decided to make up our own," Jeff says.

The result was a new body of work—a music all the Bay's own, celebrating its unique culture, history, traditions, ecology—all that makes it special. In the last twenty-five years, this body of songs has been steadily growing with writers and performers such as Tom Wisner (who was doing it long before anyone else), Bob Zentz, Al Petteway, and David and Ginger Hildebrand. Meneely's lilting ode to the Bay's string of Eastern Shore islands, which the Oyster Boys often perform, is a fine example: "Tilghman, Tangier,/Smith,

Hooper, Deal, / Steeples in the summer sky, / Lilies in the field / On your shores I'll drop my sails / I'll drop my anchor 'round / And let your comfort cover me / Till the sun goes down."

Crab Alley eventually split up, but not before Jeff had met Kevin Brooks, who was a Maryland boy born and bred and an accomplished upright bass player and sideman in the Annapolis-Baltimore-D.C. area. "I was kind of the itinerant white folk bass player who worked with a lot of groups," Kevin says. Jeff asked Kevin to accompany him on the *Woodwind* cruises, and before long, Kevin ditched the bass for a six-string banjo, creating a whole new sound for the pair. Taken together, they even *look* like a perfect team—the burly, bearded bard Jeff, with his tiny ukulele perched on his round stomach, next to the compact, athletic Kevin and his banjo.

A new partnership was born, and the two began collaborating on the songsmithing, which Kevin was anxious to try. "I was at first a little intimidated to co-write," he says, "but I've found it's easy to write about things you know and love." For instance, the three things you really need to be happy in Eastport: "Good Hat, Good Dog, Good Boat," written by Kevin in 1998. A proven crowd pleaser, this tune celebrates the simple delights of Eastport life, as told by Kevin's old friend Willie, who explains that a good hat will keep you cool when it's hot, a good dog "will stick with you through thick and thin / They won't fuss when you come home late,' Give a big kiss and then they'll shake / A good dog will be your very bestest friend." And of course—a good boat. "She will take you near and far, / When you get there, that's where you are! / A good boat is all you need to get around."

The Oyster Boys repertoire is, in a word, eclectic, both in its musical style and subject matter. "Reef Down Day," is a Caribbean rhythm, "Back Creek Crab," is a rag tune, "Sou'wester," is country-western swing, "Miss Lonesome," is a traditional acoustic piece about a beautiful old workboat that has fallen on hard times. "Subaquatic Vegetation" is a hilarious tango in E minor that uses a tongue-twisting lyric to point out one of the Bay's most critical and threatened habitats—underwater grasses. "The baby-boomer generation / Has fostered overpopulation / Waterfront property inflation / Development, deforestation / Deforestation leads to soil erosion that wreaks / Environmental devastation / On subaquatic vegetation." Whatever their topic, the songs are meant to deliver their message gently, humorously, almost subliminally, Jeff says. "The idea is to find out what it is that makes this place special and pick it out and celebrate it," he says, "and I think people realize that if something is worth singing about, it is special."

Every now and then the Oyster Boys will be joined by their Big Band, a rather itinerant and fluctuating group of musicians who number about ten and perform at larger venues. They include the Horn Point Horns and the Back Creek Backup Band. Most of the Oyster Boys' work, though, is as a duo.

They have two CDs to their credit and are working on a third, all the while keeping their "real jobs"—Kevin is executive director of the Maryland Rural Development Corporation, and Jeff owns his own public relations firm, Holland Lines, and is director of the Annapolis Maritime Festival.

In 1995, Annapolis Mayor Alfred Hopkins proclaimed Jeff the poet laureate of Eastport, noting that "using poetic license [he] has brought the history and heritage of Eastport alive in the most entertaining manner." When, in 1998, the bridge over Spa Creek connecting Annapolis to Eastport was closed for three weeks for repairs, he and Kevin were among a cadre of "Eastportoricans" who grabbed the opportunity to have some fun. They held a revolution to secede from the city, proclaiming the Maritime Republic of Eastport (MRE) its own entity, complete with its own Navy, Air Force and Declaration of Independence which entitles all MRE citizens to the rights of liberty from "suits, ties and socks" and the pursuit of "prize rockfish, the finish gun, two-week cruises, crabs, beer and oysters." Kevin came up with the MRE's slogan, written over a broken bridge on the Republic's flag: "We Like It This Way." The bridge has long since been repaired, but the MRE is more alive than ever, holding annual events and fund-raisers and creating a civic pride that has taken even its seat-of-the-bar-stool organizers by surprise.

It's no small feat to pack all that joy and laughter and culture and history into a short song and get it across to a bunch of strangers on the swaying deck of a sailboat. But beers in their pockets and songs in their hearts, Them Eastport Oyster Boys sure look like they're having fun trying. ▪

Annapolis City Dock

Annapolis, the "city of Anne," got its start in 1649 when Puritans established a settlement (which they called Providence) close by the Severn River. A half-century later, in 1708, Annapolis was officially chartered under Royal seal and named for the future Queen Anne of England. Steeped in colonial history— the Treaty of Paris, which ended the Revolutionary War, was signed here—Annapolis has always been a gateway to the Chesapeake Bay, a natural port where livelihoods, transportation, and commerce depended heavily on the surrounding waters. City Dock became a bustling arena where watermen offloaded their catches, ships were launched, and a steady stream of vessels arrived and departed laden with passengers and goods. Surrounded today by the city's charming historic district, the Dock still holds tight to its status as a thriving hub: It offers prime views of sailboat races and other festivities that celebrate Annapolis as America's Sailing Capitol, and within easy walking distance are the U.S. Naval Academy and notable buildings such as Maryland's State House—the oldest state capitol still in use in the United States.

Window on the Chesapeake

FLOWER HUNTER

Only the fitful month of March could be this ornery. The sky is an unrelenting press of gray, inhospitably spitting a frigid rain. The wind bites like an ill-tempered mutt. Beneath a wide-brimmed hat, armed only with rubber gloves, Sara Tangren is on her hands and knees in the mud. And loving it. With a small trowel, she is prying carefully into the sandy loam, searching with all the enthusiasm of a treasure hunter. "Here we go," she says, and lifts from the earth a scrawny, pale finger of a root that looks like it wanted to be a carrot but never made it past tuber pre-school.

"Butterfly milkweed. You won't believe how these will grow, and the monarch caterpillars and butterflies love 'em. A dry slope to them is like a day at the spa."

Treasures indeed are these humble little roots, for they represent all that Sara is trying to achieve in her effort to preserve, protect and propagate wildflowers born and bred of the Chesapeake Bay. At her Chesapeake Native Nursery in Davidsonville, a few miles south of Annapolis, she is doing what few others have done here—growing native wildflowers from the local ecosystem to produce native seed and seedlings. In the process, she hopes to preserve plants that are as much a part of the Bay's heritage as crabs and skipjacks—and just as threatened by a changing environment: development, pollution and other pressures. "According to historic literature, a lot of native plants were very common here, and now you can't find them," she says. "In the case of wild columbine, we went to the University of Maryland herbarium and wrote down where all those pressed specimens had been collected from the 1930s on. We went back to those sites and they had all been developed."

Sara, who has a master's degree in marine environmental sciences and a doctorate in natural resource sciences, was an environmental consultant in the late 1980s and 1990s. Developers would hire her to delineate wetlands, identify rare or endangered species—define the environmental issues their projects faced, in short, and plan how to deal with them. On some levels, it was a wonderful job; how often can you get paid to walk woods and fields and spend time in the countryside you love? On others, it made her sick. "You would see incredible places and things no one else got to see. But yet you knew they were going to get bulldozed. And when you're watching it happen, it makes you want to throw up." Wildflowers had always fascinated and pleased her; she routinely would take an identification guide along as she trekked the land. Then one day she visited a developer's site in Calvert County and came across a small population of purple-fringed orchids. The flower "is not that rare, and it's not protected by state law," she says. "But it's absolutely beautiful. At that time I lived in a condo, and I couldn't even dig them up and plant them in my lawn. There was absolutely nothing I could do. And now there's a road there. I just got sick and tired of it. So I said, we're going to lease some land and see if we can rescue some of these plants, and see if we can propagate them."

Her goal was to develop a business producing native seed from wildflowers of the Virginia and Maryland Bay watershed. Most seeds that gardeners buy at their local nurseries or garden stores come from the Midwest, Sara says, and the native seed producer closest to the Bay is in western Pennsylvania. By finding local flowers, planting them in her nursery in Davidsonville and cultivating them, she could produce seed native to Bay ecosystems and sell plants and seed to corporations, landscapers, state highway administrations and, eventually, home gardeners.

"A species can be native over a huge geographical area," she says. "Like butterfly milkweed—a gorgeous plant that's native anywhere east of the Rockies." But butterfly milkweed from Nebraska, for instance, will grow differently than butterfly milkweed from Maryland, blooming and seeding at different times and sometimes failing to thrive at all in a new region. "Until recently, if you wanted to buy butterfly milkweed you would have to buy it from the Midwest. I bought one and planted it here because I was so excited about this plant, and it died before the end of the season. So it's important to grow within the ecotype of the Bay." That's the whole point of Sara's little roots: They're "been heres," not "come heres." They like it here. It's home. Severe weather, prolonged drought, wilting humidity, poor soil, indigenous bugs, birds and pollinators—they're all factors within the Bay region to which these plants have adapted over generations. That means they're very low maintenance, rarely needing pesticides or fertilizers or even extra water.

Sara defines "native" as plants that were present before Europeans arrived in the 1600s, and she has partnered with the Maryland Department of Agriculture to develop a "source identification program." That is, the same inspectors who go out and check that farmers are, indeed, growing the seed they say they are, will also examine parent populations of wildflowers that Sara has identified and verify them, ultimately certifying the provenance of her seeds. If a parent population is in no danger, Sara gets permission from the landowner to collect seeds from the flowers to cultivate on the farm. If the bulldozers are fueling up, she gets permission from the developer to rescue as many of the plants as possible. "I've never been told no," she says. "One developer actually used his backhoes to lift whole sections of plants and set them aside for us." She finds her flowers through contacts from her former consulting business, her routine travels and hikes, and even from people who know of her work and call her to say they've spotted something she should see.

After she obtains the plants or seeds, the next step is getting them to grow, and if the two-acre garden in Davidsonville is any indication, she and her part-time employees (along with her husband, Bill) have a green thumb. Designed in a huge circle, with mulched paths shooting from the center like spokes, the nursery is now home to about forty wildflower species, among them the glowing Maryland goldenaster, the exuberant daisy fleabane, the unfortunately named purple sneezeweed (which looks an awful lot like a black-eyed Susan), the cobalt blue bottle gentian, Maryland's own indigenous cactus, the prickly pear, the elegant foxglove beardtongue and the charming pink fuzzy bean, which Sara says attracts the most exotic caterpillars in the whole place. "We get to see all the very coolest bugs, all the best bugs," she says. "That's a big motivator for what we're doing, to see the native bugs and species inter-acting with the plants. There's something neat going on with the native plants every month." For instance, she was alarmed to see caterpillars devouring the leaves on her butterfly milkweed. "They stripped the plants to sticks but we couldn't touch the caterpillars. So we said, we'll just have to wait and see. Well, the butterfly milkweed got three times as many flowers, and when they bloomed, the butterflies were just arriving and needed the nectar."

Sara started the business in 1999, and by the fall of 2001 she produced her first native seed for sale. She has sold seed to the Maryland State Highway Administration, which sowed it at the Bay Country rest stop on the Eastern Shore on Route 301. She has since sold plants and seed to the Chesapeake Bay Foundation, the U.S. Naval Observatory, the Naval Research Lab, the City of Laurel, Virginia Tech and St. John's College in Annapolis. Corporate developers have begun to call as well, and her plants have been sold at several retail nurseries. Sara predicts that as people learn about the value of the plants—both in their heritage and their easy-going ability to grow well—the idea of gardening with native plants will take off.

Her biggest challenge now, she says, is learning how to run a growing business, and still find time to get her hands dirty. "I imagine it will get to where I only get out in the field to walk through it," she says. "There is so much energy, so much positive energy when you walk through that field on a summer day." And so much more to find. Wild blue phlox, for example. She's only ever found it along the Potomac River, in a national park, so she can't touch it. She's called some friends at the Maryland Native Plant Society to keep their eyes peeled for her. She'll consult the history books, learn where it was known to grow in the past. She'll keep looking. The flower hunter shows no signs of letting the bulldozers win. ◾

William Brown House
at Historical London Town
and Garden in Edgewater, MD

Historic London Town

South of Annapolis, on the banks of the South River, horticulture and history mingle on the twenty-plus acre estate known as Historic London Town and Gardens. Residents of the seventeenth and eighteenth- century town of London in colonial Maryland—now being excavated by archaeologists—most likely had an everyday acquaintance with at least some of the native and imported medicinal plants that today grace the estate's serene eight-acre woodland garden. Managed by the London Town Foundation in cooperation with Anne Arundel County, the site also is home to the William Brown House, a National Landmark house and museum.

BOATS IN THE FAMILY

This old porch has seen a lot. You can feel it in the boards. It gazes southeast, looking across the West River where it meanders off into Lerch Creek and Smith Creek, South Creek and Johns Creek. For some 124 years this porch and the white clapboard house it fronts have perched here, enduring storm and flood and the pounding footfalls of children, watching schooners laden with timber, log canoes brimming with oysters, lithe little skiffs sailed by tanned young men and gleaming mahogany powerboats that rumble and glow. And they all came here, to the old white house—the focal point, since 1878, of Hartge Yacht Yard.

Among mariners on the middle Chesapeake Bay, Hartge's is synonymous with boats and people who know how to build, restore and repair them. Only the apple pies and sticky buns at the West River Market—just a few short blocks from the old white house—carry the small town of Galesville's fame farther, and that's probably only because apple pies and sticky buns, even extraordinary ones, are easier to come by than boats. So many of the old boatyards that once dotted the Bay's nooks and crannies are long gone, or morphed into posh "yachting centers" rife with swimming pools, weight rooms and manicured gardens. Hartge's is among the few where you can still tie up your boat, walk to the old porch and breathe the rich aroma of the past.

In a single room in the old house, the Hartge Nautical Museum encompasses some 170 years of Chesapeake and West River history, seen through the prism of the Hartge family that dug its roots so deeply here. In doing so, it reveals generations of Bay life and experience. "It's been in my mind forever," says eighty-five-year-old Laurence Hartge, the driving force behind the museum's conception and development. "Evidently I was the member of the family who drove my elders crazy because I always asked a million questions. I'm really pleased that I was so damned curious." Not until he was living in Florida, where he became a docent at the Amelia Island Museum of History, did the idea really jell. By the time he returned to Annapolis (just north of Galesville), "I had a museum in my mind. I thought, I've got a collection of all this stuff. It's a shame there isn't a museum about the Hartge Yacht Yard."

Laurence has devoted the museum largely to the boatyard's inception and early years, and to the myriad boats Hartges have designed and built. Watching the boats evolve in style and purpose, we see how the Bay and its tributaries shifted from water highways and workplaces—where trade and transportation depended upon sail, wind and water—to a place where people go for relaxation and recreation. With the help of an exhibition designer, Laurence has created a compact and professional examination of the past and its evolution to the present. Tools, vintage photographs, paintings and boat models are sprinkled throughout. Half-shell lights arrayed around the ceiling glow like mother of pearl, suspended from thin cables tightened with tiny turnbuckles, while beneath your feet, the old wooden floor creaks. Laurence says he wanted the museum to stand on its own as a unique record of the maritime past. "It's not a family thing," he says. "It's about what the family has contributed to the history of the Bay's boats."

The exhibit begins with the family's progenitors, Henry and Emile, who immigrated to Baltimore from Germany in 1832. Henry was a piano maker (one of his beautifully carved pianos occupies an entire corner of the room) who fell in love with West River on one of his many steamboat forays around the Bay. In the mid 1800s he bought 467 acres of what is now West Shady Side (a peninsula at the river's southern entrance) and set up shop.

In 1878, Henry's grandson Emile Alexander and his wife, Susan, bought a chunk of land called White Stake Point farther upstream near Galesville and constructed a home to accommodate what would become a family of eleven children. Here, Emile turned his natural-born skill in crafting wood toward boat building. "Emile really was an entrepreneur," says Laurence, his grandson. He used a marine railway and a horse named Jim to haul boats from the water onto land for work and fabricated a small workshop to support his repair business. But building boats was his forte. Some were for local watermen, others for himself to use for various trading enterprises he pursued around the Bay. To ensure a steady timber supply, Emile bought a plot of forest in St. Mary's County. Then he started churning out nearly every type of vessel common on the Bay at the time—bugeyes and schooners, skiffs and bateaux. And log canoes, which still race all summer long on the Bay's Eastern Shore. Emile built at least nine of the beautiful, slender craft between 1875 and 1905. Like most canoes then, they were used for fishing or carrying cargo, but the Hartges also raced them—a competitive streak that would blossom in the next generation with Emile's son Ernest "Dick" Hartge. One of Laurence's favorite exhibits in the museum is a gorgeous scale model of the thirty-eight-foot log canoe, *F.T. Lerch*, Emile built in 1896. "We always had sheds full of tools and ropes and stuff and I saw this thing there, and it was a mess," Laurence says of the model. "I asked Dick, 'What's the story of this?' " Dick not only told him the story, but gave Laurence the model on condition that he restore it.

Dick Hartge entered the business in 1920 and took over when Emile died in 1925. He studied drafting at the Maryland Institute of Art, and his heart clearly lay in designing and building boats, not in the everyday hauling, blocking, repairing and launching that constitutes the meat and potatoes of boatyard work. In 1934, he asked his brother Oscar (Laurence's father, who was a boat captain) to take over the daily yard work. Dick was now free to pursue his true passion, and he explored its nuances with a broad variety of craft: the fifty-foot schooner *Empress,* replicas of the *Ark* and *Dove*—the two boats that brought the first settlers to Maryland—and his magnum opus, the Chesapeake 20. These quick little daysailers, whose design Dick Hartge honed over several seasons of racing, are still competing, often in the West River not two miles from where they were created. On one wall in the museum hangs a list of all the major boats Dick built—122 is Laurence's best count, though he says there were probably more. Next to it is an identical sheet inviting visitors to note any changes or additions to the list—and several have done so.

Unlike his father's vessels, most of Dick's boats were built for recreation, not work. The Bay was changing; after World War II, the schooner trade that Emile had plied so successfully effectively died, while national boat manufacturers like Chris-Craft and Chesapeake builders like Whirlwind, Owens and CruisAlong catered to an enthusiastic and war-weary public anxious to leave work on land and find fun on the water.

That public has today made Hartge Yacht Yard one of the best known working boatyards on the Chesapeake. It continues to thrive, sprawling around the old white house, under the management of Alex Schlegel, Emile's great-grandson. The boats are mostly fiberglass, though a few glamorous old "woodies" still shimmer beneath the shelter of covered boat sheds, among them several built by Dick Hartge. Alex, who lives across Lerch Creek, drives a skiff to work in the morning, and his mother, Elsie Hartge Schlegel Wallis, still lives across the river on Chalk Point, where the steamboat used to land. His sister Elsie Whitman is an artist and partner in a terrific gallery in town, and says the family's history runs deep enough in Galesville and the West River to give its members a profound sense of belonging. "The ones who could, stayed," she says. And they can still stand on the old porch and watch the river, where the boats still pass by. ▪

THE SNEAKER INDEX

The tip of Broomes Island dips into the Patuxent River like a toe pointing due south almost halfway across the broad, sparkling water. It isn't the only thing dipping into the river today, a bright Sunday in June. There are feet in flip-flops, feet in surf shoes, feet in old boat shoes and in holey high-tops, all stepping off the white ribbon of beach on the island's eastern edge and into its sandy shallows, wading until they fade from sight. The people attached to these feet enter the water hand-in-hand led by one man—not a preacher, exactly, not a politician, necessarily, not an environmental activist, per se. Just a man who grew up here when you could wade chest-high in water clear as an ice-cold 7-Up, who has dedicated much of his life to cleaning up the Patuxent so he can wade up to his shoulders again some day and still see the toes poking from his scruffy white sneakers. "You're here today because you truly love this river," former Maryland State Senator Bernie Fowler tells the crowd of about 100 at his fifteenth yearly Senator Bernie Fowler River Community Wade, as the guest book names it. "Until the day we can truly wade out shoulder-high and see our feet in the water, nothing less will be acceptable."

Striding into the water in blue overalls and a cowboy hat, Bernie Fowler resembles a stalk of winter wheat, reedy, tall and deceptively resilient. He's seventy-eight years old now, but his passion for his home river burns stronger than ever. When he talks about the decades of battling pollution and attitudes that threaten the Patuxent and the Bay, he still gets on the edge of his chair and pounds one fist into a palm. Though his three terms as a state senator were over in 1994, he remains one of the Bay's most articulate and stalwart advocates, always being called upon by governors and scientists to chair this commission or that task force. "If all you've left behind is dirty water and dirty air for the generations, then your life has been worthless," he says in his typically blunt, heartfelt way. "That's what keeps me stimulated. I've got eight grandchildren and four great-grandchildren." True, he says, some of his motivation is ego-driven. But he flat out loves the Patuxent and isn't shy about saying so. "I just have an uncompromising love and affection for that river and the Bay. That really is the heart of Maryland, and if we were to lose the Chesapeake Bay and its tributaries, that heart would stop beating."

Wading in the water each June—an event that's part political picnic, part tent revival and baptism, part local fair—is how he reminds everyone that the

Bay still isn't out of the cardiac unit. It's a simple idea, really, to be able to see one's feet on the sandy bottom. That's the beauty of it. Talk nitrogen loads and submerged aquatic vegetation acreage, and pretty soon people's eyes glaze over. Tell them that when you grew up, you could see a crab wink twelve feet down but now you're lucky to spot one at three feet, and it's all quite clear. It was something as a youngster he took completely for granted as he netted soft-crabs, enjoying the shimmery brush of seaweed wrapping around his long legs. The river's tendrils perforated and pocked Broomes Island, and gave it its livelihood and soul. "You could gig eels in the spring of the year and see twelve feet down," Bernie says. "You could reach down and nipper oysters twelve or fourteen feet down. The [underwater] grass went out for two or three football fields." Bernie remembers his mother catching as many as twenty-five dozen soft-shell crabs in a day, and good crabbers could catch ten barrels of hard shells on trotlines. "That's not little barrels," he says, holding his hand about four feet above the floor, "that's big sugar barrels. The river was just so beautiful. What a beautiful sight that is, to be standing on top of a boat and look down and see striped bass running through the grass and the crabs down there."

But by the 1960s, the river was dying. Oyster and crab harvests were crashing and so were the economies of places like Broomes Island that had depended upon them for generations. Like a canary in a coal mine, the Patuxent was foretelling a Bay-wide problem. When Bernie ran for a seat on the Calvert County Board of County Commissioners in 1970, he was determined to learn what was happening to his home river and how to stop it. Scientists were finding that excessive nitrogen and phosphorus—largely from upstream sewage treatment plants—was causing much of the problem. Population growth was spurring development, and the river was becoming, quite literally, a toilet. "In the early 1960s we had about three million gallons a day going into the river from wastewater treatment plants. By the early 1970s, it was about thirty million gallons a day. The technology was not there. But the growth was there, and it just wore the old river down.

"I got to thinking, doggone it, we have the same right to enjoy clean water as much as they have a right to build all those homes up there," Bernie says. "We had talked to the governor, the attorney general, the EPA, and we were just not getting anywhere. I actually had one official, who shall remain nameless, say, 'You're going to chase tourists away from Maryland with all your talk of the Bay down there dying. There's nothing wrong with the Bay.' See, that was money talking then. The heart didn't go into that conversation, and they thought the Bay would go on ad infinitum. But that was money talking."

And Bernie was fed up with empty words. State Senator Roy Dyson, who now holds Bernie's seat in the Senate, remembers a meeting of the Tri-County Council for Southern Maryland (representing the river counties of Calvert, St.

Marys and Charles) when Bernie made it clear he was done with talking. "He said, 'Let's sue the state,' " Dyson recalled, laughing at how shocked the delegates were. "We said, 'You want to sue the state? Our state?' And he said, 'Yes, that will send a message.' "

Bernie Fowler (center) with fellow waders

So they did—and they sued the EPA too—in federal court in Washington, D.C., for failing to enforce provisions of the Clean Water Act. The fight was bitter and long. The work of scientists like the late Dr. Donald Heinle of the Chesapeake Biological Laboratory in Solomons, Maryland, almost cost them their jobs. But in 1979, the judge agreed with the counties and ordered federal funds for water and sewage treatment plants to be withheld until the state could develop a plan to control the pollution. Right after the decision, then-Governor Harry Hughes pledged $29 million in state aid to clean up the nitrogen from the largest plant on the river.

It was precedent-setting for the Chesapeake and the Patuxent. Yet it didn't really make people *see* how sick the river and the Bay were. So Bernie, on the advice of his folk-singer friend Tom Wisner, started wading again, this time to make a point. Begun in 1988, the annual wade has attracted hundreds of people including governors, congressmen and, in a sweet piece of irony, at least one EPA administrator. The wade results in the "sneaker index," an annual measurement from Bernie's old white high-tops to the high-water mark on his blue overalls. The EPA, which is now a major partner in the Chesapeake Bay Program, participates in and assists with the wade, and uses its results as a primary annual indicator of the state of the Bay. The index reached a shin-high low point in 1989 at eight inches and a waist-high peak in 1997, at forty-four and one-half inches.

Photograph courtesy of Sotterley Foundation

Slave cabin at Sotterley Plantation

In 2002, forty-two and three-quarters inches of Bernie—and everyone else—got soaked. The goal is fifty-seven inches.

As to whether he'll get there, Bernie admits to some doubt. As he sees it, the Bay is locked in a battle for its life with the unrelenting population growth all around it and within its watershed. He wants to see wastewater treatment plants release no more than three milligrams of nitrogen and less than one milligram of phosphorus per liter, year-round. He wants to see greater control of emissions by automobiles and industry and less runoff from commercial, residential, industrial and agricultural sources. "The acceleration of the growth will be the death of the Bay unless we somehow limit what we are doing. I know the builders and tax collectors and business owners don't want to hear that, but you can't have everything… Seeing the Bay and its tributaries as they were in the 1950s will be difficult to achieve. You really hate to even think of things like that, because when you dedicate so many days of your life, and the thousands and thousands of people who have worked so hard, certainly they're not worthy of disappointment," he says. "We've got to keep moving ahead with uncompromising determination."

As part of the wade-in this day, Bernie offers a tribute to Donald Heinle, placing a wreath in the water to commemorate the dedication of the scientist, who died in 2001. "He was first and foremost a gentleman, he was a great scientist and he stuck to his guns," Bernie says. "Because of his tenacity and courage this Patuxent River is the better for it today." No doubt, the same can be said of the tall fellow from Broomes Island who has always loved wading in the river. ■

CHESAPEAKE BAY
GATEWAYS NETWORK

Sotterley Plantation

Like so many features of the Chesapeake region, Maryland's Patuxent River is imbued with both natural beauty and historical meaning. On the river's western shore south of New Market, Sotterley Plantation illuminates eighteenth- century life along the river, where the 890-acre plantation's bustling steamboat landing played a central role in the region's economic life. Sotterley predates other, better-known Chesapeake region plantations such as Mount Vernon and Monticello. Among the treasures of the original manor house (restored in the early 1900s) are a Chinese Chippendale staircase and carved ornaments considered to be among the finest examples of eighteenth-century American woodwork. Sotterley was a working estate, however, and in the early 1800s it became the site of one of the largest slave communities in southern Maryland. A rare, well-preserved slave cabin still exists on the grounds, along with several other historical structures and a formal garden.

Julia A. "Julie" King is no Indiana Jones. She has not, in recent memory, leaped any chasms of lava, escaped marauding artifact looters on horseback or picked her way across ancient floors squirming with asps. At least, not literally. Figuratively, she may be doing all that and more in her efforts to preserve Maryland's archaeological history, and to make it as accessible as possible to everyone who might want to learn something from it. As director of the Maryland Archaeological Conservation Laboratory (MAC Lab) at Jefferson Patterson Park and Museum, Julie King doesn't need Hollywood to jazz up the field of archaeology. The MAC Lab is the finest of its kind in the country, and with her passion for the work that goes on there, Dr. King can manage just fine without Professor Jones's signature fedora and special effects.

"You can see, it's not a lot of sexy stuff. This looks like a nice iron glob here," she says, picking up an egg-sized clump of reddish-brown material, which happens to date from the eighteenth-century Catoctin Furnace—an operation that produced iron for well over 100 years. "It's not sexy, but we don't keep it because it's sexy. We keep it because it can teach us something. People think, why are you saving all these broken, rusty nails? Well, we're saving them because they have scientific and cultural significance, and we can learn from them."

The Catoctin Furnace artifacts are part of a project that says volumes about what Julie is trying to achieve. They are among about four million artifacts (nobody knows the exact number) at the Maryland Historical Trust's MAC Lab that have gone more or less untouched for decades. They come from 2,000 sites throughout the state and cover a broad swath of history, from Native American occupation to the American Revolution, Civil War and early twentieth century. For decades, these pieces of Maryland history were scattered all over the state—in basements, attics, closets and even in public storage facilities. To the layman, maybe this doesn't sound so bad, but to archaeologists and historians, it was like using the priceless family Bible to prop up a gimpy chair. "Some collections we had lost because there wasn't a good place to keep them," Julie says. "We had to face up to the responsibility of taking care of this." In the mid-1980s, the director of the Maryland

Historical Trust, J. Rodney Little, suggested to the Legislature that the state build a single place to hold all the collections, and in 1998, the $8.5 million MAC Lab, located at Jefferson Patterson Park and Museum on the Patuxent River, became a reality. (The site of the park and museum is itself an archaeological treasure, yielding Native American artifacts from the mid-1400s to items from a seventeenth-century plantation.)

That was step one. Step two is a longer leap—finding out just what all those collections hold. In 2001, the lab won a $136,000 grant from the National Endowment for the Humanities to take thirty-one of the lab's most important collections—about one million artifacts—re-catalog them, and then place that information on a website, so archaeologists and historians anywhere in the world could find it, use it, learn from it. This is what's going on in "the range," the nickname for a long, open, well-lit room that is the lab's "clean" area, where artifacts can be examined in an environmentally controlled, safe place. Tall windows face north (northern light is flatter and makes it easier to see colors accurately) and stacks of blue notebooks lining the walls are filled with the field notes that describe the artifacts' provenance. Rows of tables provide ample space for researchers, who are painstakingly extracting artifacts from the Catoctin Furnace collection—pieces of glass, ceramics, charcoal, iron, an eighteenth-century iron cooking pot, nearly intact. They examine each piece, no matter how apparently insignificant, catalogue it, rewrap it—in padded foam made of virgin polyethylene, since recycled polyethylene has chemicals that can degrade artifacts. Then they place it in a labeled plastic bag, adding some silica to suck up any moisture, and move on to the next. It's laborious, tedious and unglamorous work that is absolutely crucial, Julie says. "I like doing field work, but where you learn about the past is in the lab," she says. "We haven't even *begun* to come to grips with the information we've dug out of the ground."

Julie's focus on digging began when she was a youngster near Crofton, Maryland. "My father was an excavating contractor," she says, "and he would go out with these bulldozers and bring home this stuff, and I got really interested in it. By the time I was in tenth grade, I knew I wanted to be an archaeologist." She studied anthropology at William and Mary, did her graduate studies in anthropology at Florida State, and then got her doctorate in American Studies at the University of Pennsylvania. In 1982, she came to southern Maryland to write her doctoral dissertation on early colonial households in the state, and in 1987 she applied for the job as Southern Maryland Regional Archaeologist at Jefferson Patterson. She returned to her home state, she says, "because of my continuing deep interest in early Maryland history and the potential archaeology has for understanding that history." She's now a leader in her field.

Her domain—the MAC Lab—is an archaeologist's mecca. Beautifully designed to mimic the tobacco barns of southern Maryland, its simple, almost Shaker-style white building overlooks the Patuxent River. Inside, that simplicity of design continues with wide, open halls where visitors can examine work in progress through windows or conduct research in a spacious library.

What goes on behind the windows and doors is anything but simple. The lab's primary functions are research, conservation and collections management, and the building is more or less divvied up to accommodate those purposes. State-of-the-art equipment— and an architectural form that follows function—makes it possible to take an artifact fresh from the field, conserve and stabilize it in the main treatment lab and finishing lab, study it in labs with specialized equipment (where scientists can even analyze something as fine as pollen samples), then store it in the building's cavernous, environmentally controlled collections area, where row after row of compactable shelving on two floors house thousands of boxes of artifacts. There's even a room specially designed for working with potentially explosive chemicals while conserving or stabilizing an artifact. If something should go boom, an exterior wall will blow out, directing the explosion away from the scientist (and the artifact). The lab is one of only three facilities in the country qualified to take federal artifacts—pieces that come from federal lands or property such as naval ships.

If that all sounds rather academic, spend some time in the main treatment lab, a gigantic room dominated by a five-ton overhead crane for moving and lifting large objects. From the walls, articulated arms reach down to work tables, ending in wide funnels that suck up vapors from solvents so scientists can work closely on delicate pieces. Here, lead conservator Howard Wellman and his staff work on materials as fragile as a chunk of hawser from an eighteenth-century shipwreck to a massive oak elbow that supported ships under construction at the Steward Shipyard in Galesville, Maryland in the 1750s. Here is part of a Bibb flue, a tobacco-drying oven patented in 1861 and found in a barn right up the road, and a cannon from the *H.M.S. Nimrod*, which attacked the U.S. coast during the War of 1812. It was still loaded, Wellman says, with two sets of cannon balls wedged behind fragments of wadding and a muzzle plug. At the far end of the room is a huge silver box with a round, black door on the front. It looks like a hyperbaric chamber, but it's an enormous freeze-drier used to stabilize organic artifacts—like that oak ship brace, if it can fit.

In the next room over, the finishing lab, a fifteen-foot-long dugout canoe dating from the 1700s and found in La Trappe Creek is undergoing reconstruction. Here, too, is the enormous acorn that was placed on top of the Maryland State House dome in 1788. Made of sandwiched layers of cypress (one from each county) and sheathed in lead and copper, the acorn, while

The MAC Lab and Jefferson Patterson State Park

under conservation, has revealed the identities of generations of workmen who etched their names into the lead.

On the first Friday of every month, the MAC Lab opens up to visitors, and archaeologists and scientists take them on a behind-the-scenes tour. Public archaeology programs, where people sign on for weeks or days of actual digging and research, are another way the lab makes its work open to everyone. It's this accessibility, Julie King says, that is truly what makes the lab valuable and its work so important. "It's not about just digging," she says. "It's how to learn about a community, learn about how people lived in the past, black, white, rich, poor." ■

Jefferson Patterson Park and Museum

The MAC Lab is located at Jefferson Patterson Park and Museum, itself a remarkable state museum of history and archaeology. In 1981, Mary Marvin Breckinridge Patterson was trying to decide what to do with the 512-acre Point Farm she and her late husband, Jefferson Patterson, owned on the Patuxent River and St. Leonard Creek. As early as the 1920s, researchers had found evidence on the property of prehistoric occupation, and more recent study had uncovered clues about seventeenth-century colonial occupation, as well as direct involvement in the 1814 Battle of St. Leonard Creek, the largest naval engagement in Maryland's history. Mrs. Patterson asked Wayne Clark and Michael Smolek— now director of the park— to conduct a quick archaeological survey. In only about a week, they discovered forty-five sites encompassing 9,000 years of human history on this beautiful point of land. Appreciative of the land's historical significance, Mrs. Patterson in 1983 donated the entire property to the state to create a memorial to her husband. The Maryland Historical Trust, which operates the park and museum, has created a campus for archaeological and historic research. To date, more than seventy sites of archeological interest have been discovered on the property, and it is now on the National Register of Historic Places.

Window on the Chesapeake

Most people who approach the Calvert Marine Museum's diorama showing Solomons Island, Maryland, as it was in about 1890 study it from above. Jimmy Langley, though, drops right into a squat. "I like this view," he says. "I get down here, and it's just like you're in a real boat and you come around the island and look all the way to Strathmore Farm." He's right. From down here, you're pulled right in. A forest of bugeye and skipjack masts tangle the busy harbor's skyline. Neat, white clapboard houses perch along the slight spine of land poking into the Patuxent River. Hauled upon the ways of Thomas Moore's thriving shipyard, workboats await their call to the booming oyster harvest.

Jimmy Langley built this diorama, carved the houses and boats and tiny cows and outhouses—everything but the steamboat. That came from the hands of his late father, LeRoy "Pepper" Langley, who learned his art with wood and a lettering brush in the Solomons's shipyards, and who passed the crafts to his son. Now curator of exhibits at the museum and for seventeen years its model-maker, the younger Langley does not consider the detailed rendition of his hometown his best work; that honor he reserves for some of his models of Bay-built boats and his carvings of birds. But it captures his long romance with his community's history, a recurrent theme in his life and work.

"He has the sensibility, from having grown up in that culture, for making things just right," says Paula Johnson, curator in the History of Technology

Division of the Smithsonian's National Museum of American History, and Jimmy's former boss. "His models are terrific and very beautiful. Coming from that region and modeling boats from that region, he has a natural sense and feel for the details."

It seems to make perfect sense that Langley is now the one to preserve and pass along the knowledge of a craft whose roots, born of necessity, are long gone. His father went to work at Solomons's preeminent shipyard, M.M. Davis and Son, in the 1930s, and quickly became its top painter. Effortlessly, it seemed, he could letter in freehand the name and hailing port on the convex curve of a boat's transom or nameboard. Lettering and woodworking helped the elder Langley support a family of six in the rural, mostly poor community. His third child, Jimmy, was utterly fascinated with his father's ability.

Jimmy Langley's brushwork is striking; he has lettered about 9,000 boats over the years, and his artwork with the arcana of gold leaf keeps him in demand by yacht owners whose boats fill the marinas that have replaced Solomons's shipyards. But models are his true calling. Each one he builds to exacting accuracy. If he lacks the designer's drawings, or if he's building a boat like a skipjack which never had drawings, he measures the actual boat himself, draws the plans, makes the patterns and builds the model. "Museum work is important," he says. "You don't just sit down and chop out a generic boat." He makes everything in or on the models; working blocks as small as corn kernels, a yacht's wheel the size of a Ritz-Bitz, each needle-thin spoke clearly delineated. Each model is built precisely as the boat was: Keel up, frame by frame, plank by plank, using the wood specified in the builder's plans—mahogany, pine, teak, cherry, oak. Even the grain in the wood Jimmy chooses is to scale. "Rather than three or four grains in a piece of quarter-inch wood, there might be twenty grains, real fine. So it looks like an actual piece of wood that would have been in there, rather than a piece of wood with, like, two grains, which you know is not possible."

Jimmy has built about seventy-five boat models over the years, many of them on display at the museum. His favorite is a Hooper Island draketail, an indigenous Chesapeake design that's narrow as a stiletto and notorious for eluding police during the rum-running years. His model, half-inch to the foot, is built of cherry. It looks so light and quick, you expect it to fly from its stand. Typical of his later models, Jimmy left one side and part of the deck unplanked so you can examine the intricacies of the original boat's design and construction.

Jimmy attributes his fascination with carving and lettering to his father and to growing up in a town that, until the late 1970s, was nearly cut off from the rest of the world. Until the Governor Thomas Johnson Bridge was built over the Patuxent, turning Solomons into a tourist destination, the little town near the river's mouth was pretty much dead, at least from a young boy's point of view. It was better than an hour's drive to the nearest outpost like a

McDonald's, and although a boat could dash you across the river to St. Mary's County, there wasn't much going on there, either. But there was always something happening in Pepper Langley's workshop. "I remember from three or four years old I'd go out and set in a corner," Jimmy says, "and he had a little bench over there and he'd give me a handful of nails and a hammer and a piece of wood, and every fifteen minutes or so you'd hear 'Oooh,' and he would look around and know I'd smacked my thumb." True to form, though, Pepper wouldn't say much about it, just reckon that his son would eventually figure out the right way to do things. At that time, Jimmy says, his father was lettering names onto boats and ships nearly fulltime. To his young son, it was pure magic. "I was astounded that he could take a brush and dip it in paint and hold it by the end and create what seemed to be a perfect 360-degree circle. Freehand. And completely ruler-straight lines… I guess I envied him, and every opportunity I had I was in his workshop."

By the time he was about eleven, his dad put him to work. A nearby beach club had about thirty signs with its logo—a woman diving out of some art-deco clouds wearing a full-piece bathing suit—that needed to be repainted twice a year. "They all had yellow bathing suits. I can show you today what that bathing suit looked like," he says, grabbing a piece of paper and sketching a quick outline. When his father eventually quit lettering, tired of being constantly on call to the boatyards, the boatyard owners starting calling the son who'd always been at his side, helping. "I guess they figured, 'He can do it,'" Jimmy says. "And could I do it? No. I couldn't letter." It took his hands months to acquire the kinetic know-how of doing. "You need to know where your hand's going when you're lettering. You don't look where you are. You look where you're going to be. So your hand is following where your eyes are kind of pointing," he says.

Carving came more easily. As with all of his art, necessity drove the work; he wanted to go duck hunting. He had no money for decoys, but his dad's shop was full of wood. Entranced with birds, pretty soon he was carving owls and snow geese and herons, along with his ducks. Eventually Jimmy got a full scholarship to one of the country's premier art schools, Maryland Institute College of Art in Baltimore, but after a year, bored and homesick, he quit. He returned to Solomons, worked for a while painting signs, and lettered and carved on the side. When the position opened up for model-maker's apprentice at the Calvert Marine Museum, where Pepper Langley was now the carver in residence, Jimmy jumped at it. His first job was to build a model of a Potomac River dory. His father was building a fishing boat called *Eleanor M.* "We set at that table in [the model shop] for nine months, each of us," he says, "and built the models."

As curator of exhibits, Jimmy isn't building many boat models these days, but he continues to carve. In his bright office, he pulls from under his desk

Drum Point lighthouse

Calvert Marine Museum

In the 128-year old waterfront village of Solomons, Maryland, Calvert Marine Museum vividly illuminates life—plant, animal, and human—in and around the Chesapeake estuary. Fifteen aquaria, the largest holding 3,500 gallons, assemble a panoply of the creatures that inhabit the Bay's salt and brackish waters as well as the upper Patuxent. Four centuries of human enterprises along the Patuxent are called up like friendly ghosts by 500-plus artifacts, including a three-log canoe. Tucked into a protected cove, Calvert also lays claim to two lighthouses, one offshore at Cove Point and the on-site Drum Point lighthouse, a screw-pile structure that once guided Bay mariners past shoals at Drum Point. A classic Chesapeake bugeye, the *Wm. B. Tennison*, regularly departs the Museum's pier with sightseers—another avenue for exploring the Calvert's well-put-together blend of Bay ecology and maritime history.

a mahogany box with brass corners and latch. He opens the front to reveal three small sliding shelves piled with hand tools—broad chisels of polished high-carbon steel from Switzerland, tiny knives for the intricate tips of a heron's wing, tools he made from some of Pepper's old straight-razors. He turns them over in his hands, describing the provenance of his favorites. He loves the work and the medium, and all that they connect him to. "Wood is so beautiful. And you think, every little one of those lines that you see in wood is a year. And here you are, into this piece of ninety-year-old wood that was here fifty years before I was born." He shakes his head in wonder. "Who knows what was going on, or who walked under that tree?" ■

SMALLWOOD'S RETREAT

It was called a retreat, and even today, some 240 years after William Smallwood occupied its modest rooms, one can see why. In the spring, dogwoods and cherry trees flutter blossoms across the broad, sloping lawn like confetti. A warm sun floods the window into the study, where one imagines the Revolutionary War general, Maryland's fourth governor, penning letters to his friend up the Potomac, George Washington, and every now and then raising his eyes to gaze out past the boxwoods to the fields beyond. In Smallwood's time, he could clearly see the Potomac River to the west and Mattawoman Creek to the north. Today, tall banks of hardwoods obscure the view, their roots burying the shards and bones of the past.

History doesn't offer us much in the way of knowing General William Smallwood. As Ross M. Kimmel, supervisor of cultural resources for Maryland's Forest and Park Service, points out in his booklet *In Perspective: William Smallwood*: "Surprisingly little is known about his personal life. He never married, and thus left no direct heirs to help perpetuate his memory. If he kept records of his correspondence, as most men of his time and stature did, those records have been lost to posterity." But we do know that he stood here on this hill overlooking the Potomac and Mattawoman, and that he took some solace and peace from the place. That much remains clear.

The home called Smallwood's Retreat, located in the 628-acre Smallwood State Park near La Plata, Maryland, is actually a painstaking restoration. Orginally built around 1760, by the 1950s it was little more than a brick foundation. In 1958, the Smallwood Foundation rebuilt and refurnished it, basing its work upon the home's remaining bricks, records and lists of its contents. The paneling over one fireplace is original to the house, as are three of the dining room chairs. The rest of its furnishings and appointments are from the same period; the wide-plank pine floors, stairway and dining room corner cabinets, for instance, come from a Colonial-era home in St. Mary's County that was demolished.

Unlike most plantation homes, which tend toward the ostentatious, Smallwood's house is small, compact, understated and elegant. The Flemish bond brickwork—extremely sturdy construction typical of the time—creates a subtle pattern of color and texture. Two chimneys on either end are comple-mented by narrow dormers jutting from the steeply sloped roof. Inside, efficient elegance remains the rule. A centerline hallway runs north to south, the better to funnel cooling breezes in summer. The great room, where Smallwood entertained his guests, dominates the downstairs. Behind it, facing south with a cozy fireplace in one corner, is the study. Across the hallway is the dining room, and behind it is the warming room, the only fully paneled room in the house, where food would be brought from the kitchen (separate from the main house) and held until serving. From the hallway, a steep flight of stairs leads to a guest room, where fifteen people could sleep, often sitting next to one another in the bed with their backs against the wall—a typical sleeping arrangement of the time, according to Nancy Stickel, the park's director of volunteer services, who takes a special interest in learning about obscure Colonial customs. ("Sleep tight, don't let the bedbugs bite," also stems from this time, she says, when bedbugs lived in the straw mattresses, and a hand crank on the corner of the bed frame tightened the ropes that supported the mattress and sleepers). Smallwood's bedroom faces south, and behind (over the warming room below) is a small dressing room. The kitchen is just off the home's west side, and it is a complete reproduction. Stickel says the Smallwood Foundation is not certain where the original was, but the current location makes sense, based on the layout of the dining and warming rooms. The foundation has not allowed any archaeological digs at the site, she says, so the land around the house still guards its secrets.

On this land William Smallwood operated a plantation that in its heyday in the 1780s comprised some 4,000 acres, much of it leased to tenants. By 1790

Smallwood had fifty-six slaves who produced tobacco, grain, corn and wheat and maintained large herds of cattle and sheep. Smallwood's ample inventory of horses leads Kimmel to speculate he may have bred them, "a profitable sideline among the horse-happy gentry of the Chesapeake."

Smallwood was born in 1732 (the same year as George Washington), into an established, well-landed family in Maryland's Charles County. His father, Bayne, presided over the Charles County Court, Kimmel writes, and represented the county in the colony's General Assembly. Politics, wealth and land, then, were part of Smallwood's world from the start. "From the moment of their births," says Kimmel, "William and his siblings were destined to lives of wealth and social position. But in the American colonies much was expected from those to whom much was given." In William's case, public service began in 1761 when he was elected to his father's seat in Maryland's Assembly. By 1774, with the winds of revolution blowing in the colonies, Smallwood was chosen to represent Charles County at a provincial convention in Annapolis to deal with the brewing crisis. Kimmel makes an interesting point about "revolutionaries" like Smallwood: "Smallwood and his associates persisted in casting themselves as the defenders of the old and cherished order of things, not as repudiators of the established order. This, then, may be the central paradox of the American 'Revolution.' In its final outcome, at least, the Revolution was led by men of property, with stakes in the constitutional order of things, men like William Smallwood who would have much to lose in a real social revolution."

Smallwood's revolutionary fame came as colonel of the Maryland Battalion, an infantry of nine companies. In July 1776, the battalion joined Washington's forces in New York. Ironically enough, Smallwood was away on court-martial duty when the Maryland troops saw their first action in the Battle of Long Island. There, they almost single-handedly defended the American line against a superior British force, earning Maryland its nickname "The Old Line State." "Washington was to find throughout the war that his Maryland regulars were among his most reliable soldiers," Kimmel notes. Smallwood was wounded in the Battle of White Plains; Congress commended his conduct with a promotion to brigadier general.

After the Revolution, Smallwood helped form and became president of the Maryland Society of the Cincinnati, which represented the state in the group's national organization, led by Smallwood's friend and Potomac River neighbor, George Washington. (The Smallwood Foundation in 1999 helped the county purchase a letter Washington wrote from Mount Vernon to Smallwood dated December 28, 1783, announcing the group's inaugural meeting in May 1784 in Philadelphia; a replica is on display at Smallwood's Retreat.) In 1785 Smallwood was elected to Congress, and the state's General Assembly asked him to be governor. He served three one-year terms. In 1791 he was elected to the state Senate and named its president. A year later, at age sixty, he died while traveling in Prince Georges County, apparently, Nancy Stickel says, of pneumonia. In accordance with his wishes, he was buried in an unmarked grave on the hillside just west of his retreat, overlooking the Mattawoman River. In 1898 The Maryland Society of the Sons of the American Revolution erected a huge granite monument at the site—and there the enigmatic Smallwood rests, quiet amid the dogwoods, in a place that still offers solace and peace. ▪

Smallwood State Park

By way of its fifty-slip Sweden Point Marina on Mattawoman Creek, Smallwood State Park offers boaters, canoeists and kayakers ready access to the Potomac River just a mile downstream. On shore, a two-mile nature trail winds through the hardwood forest that shelters William Smallwood's treasured retreat, picnicking and camping facilities beckon, and a twenty-six mile bike trail begins its meander through the surrounding countryside— all less than an hour's drive from Washington, D.C.

WORKBOAT HERO

One of the first things you notice when you pull up to the barn at Herb Carden's place is what's hanging over the door. Weathered and worn, its rotten edges splintered, it looks remarkably like the transom of a boat. Which it is. *Wilma Lee*, it says, Tilghman MD. You can still see the blood-red bottom paint, the blue waterline stripe, the cracking white hull paint under the black letters. Beneath it, poking out of the barn doors like a long finger beckoning you inside, is the bowsprit of the sixty-two-year-old Chesapeake Bay skipjack of the same name. Tucked safely into the barn,

Wilma Lee now has a new transom—and will soon have a new life—but her old rear end is up over the barn door as something of an inspiration, and a reality check.

"I think it's important in life that you never forget where you come from, and that reminds us where we come from," says Carden. "Every time I get discouraged about the time this has taken, I come out and look at the transom and I say, 'Baby, we *have* come a long way.'"

Carden can walk out these barn doors, inhale the crisp, piney air and know exactly where he comes from: this sandy dirt, these tall loblollies, these white beaches at the confluence of the Potomac and Yeocomico rivers on Virginia's Northern Neck. He's what they call in these parts a "been here," someone who has dipped his toes in the clear waters of this place for a lifetime. His parents arrived from Richmond in 1938 as summer people and soon settled in permanently. His father, Robert C. Carden Jr., started Potomac Supply Corporation in nearby Kinsale, Virginia, at first building wooden children's toys and shipping crates for local fishermen. Soon the elder Carden began providing building supplies for other "come heres" to build their summer cottages along the Potomac and Yeocomico shores. Before long, building supplies became Potomac Supply's primary business, and it has flourished. Herb Carden is now chairman and CEO of the business, which occupies 175 acres and now has its own sawmill, planer mill, wood-treating facility and trucking division.

Growing up along some of the Bay's most lovely and historic shores and running a thriving business has created in Herb Carden a singular sort of philanthropist; he may very well be the Chesapeake's greatest unsung workboat hero. He's mad about them—crab scrapes, skipjacks, dories, skiffs— and he's made it his mission to choose a select few and find for them a new life. He wants to ensure them a future other than the bleak and likely prospect of popping a plank and sinking some bitter winter morning, or being hauled ashore and left to die quietly in the eelgrass and marshy silence. "I always loved the water and boats," says Carden as he sits along a bulkhead overlooking the sparkling Yeocomico, swinging his feet like a kid as he talks. In the distance a workboat grumbles in the glittering sun, its cockpit stacked with crab pots. "I got my first boat and motor when I was four years old. I think a boat can teach a kid more self-confidence than anything I know. Just a small skiff with a motor, and you get into situations and you have to get out of them."

Being on the water naturally meant watching the workboats and watermen working through the seasons for oysters, crabs, clams, fish. It was a life Carden always viewed from the outside. He laughs at the small irony that he has never worked a single day on the water. But the innate, tough beauty of the Bay's workhorse fleet always charmed and fascinated him, even when he was young, and he hated to see them mulching hopelessly into oblivion. "I would see these old boats as a small kid, sunk and abandoned, and I would find myself always trying to bail them out. I like the older things. I don't like trendy stuff."

As he grew older, Carden's affection for traditional boats matured into a full-blown love affair when he finally convinced a longtime neighbor and marina owner, the late Earl W. Jenkins, to sell him a Smith Island crab skiff Herb had coveted for twenty-five years. From that point on, Carden became something of a workboat humane society. People would call him and offer their old boats, hoping he would bring them to his place under the pines to await eventual restoration.

About eight years ago, he met John Morganthaler, a carpenter and shipwright from Long Island who came to Kinsale to help friends build a trimaran. Carden hired him to finish the interior of a new building, and once he saw Morganthaler's talent, he took him on full-time to work on his abandoned darlings. "John's an artist, you know, not a carpenter," says Carden. "He's taught me so much I didn't know. He does the majority of the work and I try to supply him with everything he needs in materials. And being in the lumber business has made it possible."

A tour through Carden's immaculate boathouse notched in a cove just inside the Yeocomico's mouth is like discovering a workboat exhibit in a

forgotten corner of the Smithsonian. Here's a Smith Island skiff, skinny as an arrow and beautifully finished. There's a Potomac River dory owned and built locally, impeccably restored. "That man worked that boat for years and supported his family from it," Carden says with wonder in his voice. Over here is *Little Doll*, a 28-foot crab scrape built on Smith Island by Leon Marsh and made moderately famous for carrying William Warner through the long blast furnace of a day that he recounts in his Pulitzer Prize-winning book *Beautiful Swimmers*. Broad and flat as a tea saucer and plumb of bow, this gorgeous piece of Bay culture is Carden's favorite. And way back beneath the pines, under the beat-up old transom over the barn door, is the restoration of the moment, *Wilma Lee*. Built in 1940 in Cambridge, Maryland., by Bronza Parks, the hefty girl is fifty feet long on deck and sixteen feet six inches wide.

The desire to restore a skipjack hit Herb Carden the moment he stepped aboard the *Claud W. Somers*, now a floating exhibit at the Reedville Fishermen's Museum. "I think it was in 1980," he says. "Something happened, I don't know what, and gosh, I wanted one so bad I could taste it." He and Morganthaler— along with apprentices Brian Clark and James P. Smith—got a handful in the *Wilma Lee*. Her rotted transom is a testament to the nearly complete overhaul that has taken about two years to finish. Carden plans to use the boat to teach history and Bay culture. "I want her to be used to educate the young people about the Bay itself and how things used to work," he says. "I want to do good things with her, meaningful things, something I can share with people."

Straying from traditional restoration, Carden has powered the boat with twin diesels (true working skipjacks are powered only by sail, with a yawlboat for pushing when needed) and has fiberglassed over her decks, coated her replanked hull in epoxy and rebuilt the interior cabins to be as plush as possible—never a prerequisite in a working boat. The boat's original, massive heart-pine keelson is intact; you can still see the builder's shaping marks in it. The boat's pine mast step is original as well, as is its hefty oak stem. The rest can only be defined as a labor of love, or perhaps, Carden admits, well intentioned madness. "This is where I'm crazy," he says. "The stuff I do, it would be so much cheaper to just start from scratch and just throw these boats away. But I can't throw them away." How fortunate for some good old boats. ■

Potomac Water Trail

The Yeocomico is but one of dozens of large and small waterways feeding the tidal portion of the Potomac River— waterscapes and onshore sites that travelers on the Potomac River Water Trail can explore by canoe, kayak, or small boat. Stretching nearly 100 miles from Washington, D.C., to the river's mouth, the Water Trail presents a remarkable blend of shimmering open water, quiet inlets, wildlife, and historic sites. And a lot of history began or was made along these shores: Settlers founded the colony of Maryland and later built the colony's first capitol, St. Mary's City. George Washington built his Virginia estate overlooking the Potomac at Mt. Vernon. Downriver are Washington's birthplace and Stratford Hall, the Virginia home where Robert E. Lee spent his youth. And so on, past Piney Point lighthouse to Point Lookout, where the Potomac finally opens into Chesapeake Bay. No matter which of the Trail's public launch sites marks the beginning or finale of a river traveler's journey, the destination will always be a special place.

TINY TOWNS AND OLD RIVERS

There are places on the Chesapeake Bay where you want to get lost—literally, metaphorically, certainly historically and maybe even spiritually. Lewisetta General Store is one of these. Truth be told, you almost *have* to get lost just to find it. Not by boat, so much; perched as it is by deep water at the entrance to Virginia's Coan River, just off the Potomac, the store is perfectly located for waterborne traffic, which it has seen for over a century—schooners, skipjacks, steamboats, fishing boats, you name it. By land, however, you drive down the northern side of Virginia's Northern Neck a long way before you make a left on Lewisetta Road and follow it past soybean fields and saltmarsh until it ends, with very little fanfare, in a tidy loop around the store. Which is to say, at the water's edge.

From here, you can gaze across the mouth of the mighty Potomac River, and on clear days the horizon bends away from your eye, so incoming ships and boats seem to float upon a quivering sea of light. The store's cement front porch faces southwest, looking across the Coan River, and on a sunny fall or winter day it's not just a porch—it's a Zen-like experience. It's a way to spend an afternoon meditating on tiny towns and old rivers, a way to get yourself lost for a time.

This is what Helen Scerbo does some afternoons, before the school bus winds down the road and deposits her son and daughter at the store's doorstep. She and her husband, Mark, bought the general store as part of Lewisetta Marina fifteen years ago after leaving Sandy Hook, New Jersey. At seven-and-a-half acres, they bought pretty much the whole point of land. Their house is across the street on one side of the store, the marina across the street on the other side. They've added a building for indoor boat-work, and the place has a fuel dock and slips for all sorts of boats—and even a few hookups for motor homes and RVs owned by customers who want to stay awhile. Understandably.

The store is the focal point—of the town as well as the marina. Everyone comes here for their morning coffee, or for thick deli sandwiches at lunch, or to sit on the porch on a summer's evening and trade news, gossip, fishing know-how and dime-store philosophy. And though there are only about eight full-time families in Lewisetta, the store's reputation has spread far beyond the town's modest borders.

The gray clapboard store that stands today was built in the mid-1800s. From the late 1800s until 1990, it served as the town's post office. In fact, it gave the town its name—a simple anagram of Etta Lewis, who, with her husband, Charlie, owned the store when the post office was established. Or so the story goes. In those days general stores dotted the waterfront all over the Bay, many of them linked to the steamboat lines that traversed the Chesapeake and its tributaries transporting everything from tomatoes and watermelons to livestock and people. It was far easier to travel by water in many places—the Northern Neck among them—because the water was so much more dependable than the roads, if there *were* roads. Waterways were highways, and general stores were the 7-Elevens of the time. Only a few remain, though, Lewisetta one of them. "That's the story of Lewisetta," says Scerbo, sighing. "I love Lewisetta."

"Don't forget the General Eisenhower story!" yells an elderly customer as he leaves the store. That story, says Scerbo, goes like so: One cold February morning in 1992, John D. Eisenhower, younger son of President Dwight Eisenhower, showed up at the store to relive some old memories. Back in July 1957, when his father was president and he was an Army major stationed at Fort Belvoir, he and a friend hopped in a fifteen-foot skiff and headed down the Potomac, their ambitious destination Fort Monroe in Hampton, Virginia. As the story goes, the weather riled up, and the pair more or less washed up at the Lewisetta General Store, hoping to find a room for the night. They did, just down the street at the home of Miss Olga Eubanks, who never knew that half the United States Secret Service was frantically searching for the young men. (That's the story, although truth be told, John Eisenhower says, the weather was fine, it was just getting late, and the Secret Service wasn't even assigned to him then.) It all ended well, but John Eisenhower apparently never forgot the place. He returned thirty-five years later, and he's visited several times since—giving the townspeople a hefty name to drop when the situation calls for it.

The store you see nowadays is not significantly different than what Major Eisenhower encountered in the 1950s. Over the double front door is LEWISETTA GENERAL STORE written in white cursive letters. A single, naked light bulb dangles over the porch, and the wooden screen doors slam in that particular way that makes you think of hot, buggy summer nights. Inside, the old pine floor is hidden beneath blue and white linoleum. A command center of sorts stands in the middle, holding the cash register, the kids' book bags, boxes of candy bars and arts and crafts projects to keep young fingers and minds occupied on rainy days, among them some oyster shells decorated in gold and silver paint. Behind the central counter stands a furnace with a stove pipe leading to a chimney; doubtless in decades past this spot held a woodstove where chilly hands were gratefully warmed. Hanging from the deli counter in the back is a hand-lettered sign: "MARK, PLEASE DO NOT SPILL YOUR COFFEE ALL OVER THE FLOOR. THANK YOU."

True to its roots and its name, the general store can handle most of a visitor's problems and needs. Here you will find antifreeze, fuel hoses, steering fluid, carburetor and choke cleaner, bilge pumps and the kits to repair them, electrical connectors, epoxy and boat batteries. You will also find Aunt Jemima's pancake mix, tins of Old Bay seasoning, Clorox, honey buns, toothpaste, soup, bread, Ivory soap, mustard, diapers and mayonnaise. And that hardly covers it. Scerbo has included a little bit of New Jersey humor in the T-shirts she had printed up that say: "You Almost See It All at the Lewisetta Mall."

Sitting out on the porch, Debi Wigfield, a native of Niagara Falls, New York, who moved here three-and-one-half years ago and helps Scerbo run the store (it's open seven days a week, year-round), shakes her head and laughs as the kids rough-house nearby. "It's funny how people find this place, it really is," she says. She and her husband were looking for a place to live, and he brought her down this little road till it looped around the store. "I never saw the house. I saw the marina and the boats and the water and the store," she says. "I didn't care if the floors were falling in. I was living here." The store is all about people, she says. "The men come in and they want to talk about bait and what they're catching, and I love that. I sympathize about the gas prices—of course, we have to pay it, too. You *never* get bored."

As the late-day sun warms the porch, Mark Scerbo walks up from the marina with one hand wrapped around the tails of three whopping bluefish, a gift from a customer. "Hi honey, I'm home," cracks a regular who's lounging on the porch. The sun will set soon, over the river. Maybe some dolphins will come in to play. The kids will tussle on the grass. The Lewisetta General Store will shut its doors for the night and rest awhile, awaiting the sunrise, fresh coffee and another timeless day. ■

"This is my father's world." The simple, gentle notes of the hymn rise over the crowd of a few hundred, who take up the words and carry them forward. "I rest in me the thought/Of rocks and trees, of skies and seas/His hand the wonders wrought." The voices rise into a robin's egg sky and float on the breeze across Cockrell Creek, where dozens of boats wait quietly for the words and prayers that will bless the fleet of menhaden ships from Reedville, Virginia, set to begin their season of fishing tomorrow, as they have for generations. These voices have a sweetness, a vulnerability, for they belong to those who stay behind, waiting. Not so, the songs of those who went to sea.

"WON'T YOU HELP ME RAISE 'EM BOYS!"

"Won't you help me raise 'em boys!" The voice of Calvin Hill, so soft and shy around strangers, rings like a gong over the silenced crowd, roaring with a kind of breathless urgency. "Hey, hey," comes the long, drawn-out response of the three men flanking him. "Won't you help me raise 'em boys!" Hill calls again, and the men sing together, "See you when the sun goes down," pulling the last word into a long, groaning syllable. These are members of the Northern Neck Chantey Singers, former fishermen who sing the work songs born on the Chesapeake Bay's menhaden boats to help strong men do the back-breaking work of hauling in nets loaded with hundreds of thousands of writhing fish. The four men are in their sixties and seventies; some of them move as if the weight of the loaded nets still pulls them down. But their voices are rich, as deep as an ocean and moving with the relentless power of an ebb tide on a full spring moon. They are probably the last men who will know these songs and this rhythm. So they keep singing. "They got a few tapes so it won't die out that way," Hill says. "But it'll die out as far as the men are concerned, because they can't do it no more."

When the songs were sung for work, these were young, muscular men, signed on for the season from May through October to labor in the great menhaden fleet out of Reedville. Located on Cockrell Creek off the Great Wicomico River, Reedville owes its name and its early livelihood to Captain Elijah Reed, who sailed his two small schooners from Maine to Virginia in 1867 in search of more fish and fewer fishermen. He eventually settled in what would become Reedville and established a new factory in 1874 to "cook" or process menhaden—fish he called pogies, also known locally as bunkers. The bony, largely inedible fish were easy to catch, and once rendered they were valuable for their oil and as fertilizer. It wasn't long before others joined Reed, and by the turn of the century, the little town on the tip of Virginia's Northern Neck was rolling in wealth. Ship captains built beautiful Victorian homes that today grace the town's tree-lined streets like lovely old ladies dolled up in sun hats and pearls. The reek of cooking fish was the smell of money, and every spring the boats would head out, fishing in the Bay, then up the coast off Delaware, New Jersey, Long Island and even Down East.

By the late 1800s, fishermen had established a method of catching menhaden that's fundamentally the same as the one used today. Schooners or sloops would set out armed with two oar-powered purse boats, a drive boat and a net called a purse seine. Lookouts would spot the schools of bunker and a crewman called a striker would dash out in the small, nimble drive boat to mark the school's location, often striking the water with an oar to herd the fish. The men would launch the two purse boats and, starting at the same point, methodically encircle the school with the net. As the net came full circle and was joined, a man would drop a "tom"—a heavy weight—that would close the net's bottom, imprisoning the fish within the "purse." The mother ship would come alongside and, along with the purse boats, form a triangle with the net in the middle. Then the hard work of raising the fish would begin.

In his book *The Men All Singing*, John Frye writes that chanteys weren't used on the menhaden boats at first, since the boats and catches were relatively small and the fish could be scooped from the net into the schooner with a hand-lifted dip net. But by the late 1800s, as steam engines replaced sails, vessels grew larger and engines could be used to power winches to hoist the dip nets. The nets got bigger too, as did the catches. The purse boats began carrying dozens of men who could do the arduous work of slowly raising the net and gathering in the fish, which would then be dipped out.

The work was brutal, and to help them find the extra strength to pull the nets, the men in the purse boats—mostly African Americans by the 1920s—fell back on a trusted ally, music. According to the Virginia Folklife Program, which produced a tape of the Northern Neck Chantey Singers ("See You When the Sun Goes Down") for the Reedville Fishermen's Museum, the songs derived from African American work-song tradition used in lumbering and mining. The songs were structured as call-and-response, with the leader pitching out a line and the men answering together as they pulled. The urgency was clear—if they couldn't raise the net, they'd lose the set, the fish and ultimately the income. "The chantey was when you got alongside the big boat and pursed the net," says Calvin Hill. "Chanteys helped everyone work together." William Hudnall, who organized the Northern Neck Chantey Singers in 1991, says chanteys were called when it seemed no one could pull harder and the net wasn't moving. "Somebody hit that chantey, and started to get into it," he says on "See You When the Sun Goes Down." "After awhile you see, here it starts coming up. Inch by inch. Inch by inch … You hadn't killed them and they hadn't killed you. But it was fifty-fifty—you were nearly dead and so were they." Frye quotes Reedville Captain John B. Lowry who recorded some of the songs as the men worked. "When they got together good," Lowry said, "they pulled about everything on earth."

The songs frequently addressed a topic near and dear to any young man's heart—women. "They made up songs of their own—whatever helped make a man pull," Calvin Hill says. "Most of the time they were singin' about girls." In fact, he says laughing, first thing the chantey singers as a group had to do was clean up some of their lyrics. "You can't put the real thing out there."

By the 1960s, hydraulic blocks had replaced muscle to raise the nets. As the fishery has evolved, pumps are now used to suck the fish from the nets straight into a ship's hold, inboard engines power the purse boats rather than oars, and spotters in airplanes tell the ships where to find the fish. As the need for the men's brute strength waned, so did the chanteys. "Now they just crane 'em in the whole boat," Hill says. "Plenty changes done made. Sad. Ain't got the bull work to it now, you know, muscle."

When William Hudnall first organized the singers in 1991, he found thirteen former fishermen willing and able to recall the songs and record and perform them. As time has gone on, their numbers have dwindled; their average age is seventy-five, Hill says, and it's tough to get them all together to practice for a performance. Still, a few of them gather every May at the Blessing of the Fleet, where the ships are now steel gray giants but remain vulnerable to the whim and dubious fortune of the water. "I thought I heard my baby say, she won't be home tomorrow." Under the sweet blue sky, their voices roll out like flood tide in the night, dark and enduring. "Bye-bye, bye-bye, in the hold below." ■

Photograph courtesy of Reedville Fishermen's Museum

Reedville Fishermen's Museum

Reedville was a center of the Bay's historic menhaden fishery, a past that reverberates in the gingerbread Victorian homes of Main Street and other, more modest dwellings evocative of the waterman's way of life. Fittingly, Reedville's oldest house, the William Walker House built in 1875 on the banks of Cockrell Creek, has been transformed into the Reedville Fishermen's Museum. The land on which the simple, two-story white clapboard dwelling stands once was owned by Captain Elijah Reed, the Maine fisherman who ventured south in 1867.

The museum's displays of antique Chesapeake Bay fishing implements and models of classic Bay fishing boats are contained within the Walker House and a newer structure next door. At the museum's pier the skipjack *Claud W. Somers* and a fifty-five-foot restored pound netting boat, the *Elva C*, tug at their lines—irresistible invitations to explore an authentic corner of Bay lore.

Window on the Chesapeake

THE FUSSIN' CAPTAIN

The ten members of the fishing charter party, who have driven half the night to reach Locklies Marina on time, are busy. They are loading coolers with ice and sodas, buying bloodworms and squid up at the marina store, sipping coffee and, in some cases, beer, laughing and talking and ribbing one another. What they're *not* doing is getting on the boat. The sun has been bronzing the Rappahannock River for half an hour. Daylight's burning. Captain Buddy Muse, who has seen this before, ambles up to the helm of *Ginger II* and says under his breath, "I know how to get 'em on." He turns the key and *Ginger II*'s Detroit Diesel snarls under its engine box in the center of the boat's long cockpit, water spraying from its exhaust pipes against the bulkhead where most of his party are dawdling. They leap aboard, and after a moment Muse turns the engine off. The captain has their rapt attention. "I am required by the Coast Guard to give you a brief orientation before we venture out onto the water," he says gravely. He explains how to use the fire extinguishers. He tells everyone he's sure they won't go for an unexpected swim because they will keep their feet right here, and he stamps the gray plywood of the cockpit floor. He shows where the lifejackets are stowed. Then he explains how to call for help on the VHF radio if something should happen to him. He does not smile. "All right," he says after a moment, "I guess we can go fishin'."

"Captain?" a voice pipes up from the back of the boat. "I have a question." Ten heads swing toward Lena, a legal secretary with fingernails like gold-flecked talons and a monster bass leaping across her T-shirt. One hand already has a fistful of cold Bud and a cigarette. She smiles sweetly. "If something happens to you, can I have this boat?"

Captain John "Buddy" Muse, seventy-two, serious as a heart attack about his boat and everyone on it, a man who keeps his own counsel and takes his own path, bursts out laughing for a good long time. "Well," he finally says, "you'll have to talk to my wife about that." He fires up the diesel, slips the lines and *Ginger II* heads out for a day of croaker fishing with her party, who might just be all right after all.

All around *Ginger II*, a similar ritual is happening. It begins nearly every morning between April and December, well before first light, when the charter captains gather outside the store at Locklies Marina. By 5 a.m., the place is already humming, the men's low, clipped voices telling stories and discussing the weather. One or two are already onboard, doing some last-minute cleaning or repairs. Marina owner Jack Mazmanian sips coffee and joins in the quiet banter that mingles with birdsong lifting on a warm land breeze, while Eleanor Cash, who you just *know* will call you "Hon," prunes the potted geraniums on the deck with a pair of red bolt cutters almost longer than her legs. No one bats a lash at her tool of choice. The talk this morning seems to be mostly about the weather, which rumor has it was pretty wild with

thunderstorms down near Gloucester and up to Richmond. The captains fret that their parties will cancel. "I had a no-show yesterday," says Muse. "Called him at seven-thirty and he was still in bed." The other men snort disgustedly. "So I got a special book I put him in."

Buddy Muse, Wynn Simpson, John Holmes, Bill Alestock, Joseph Thornton, Arthur Kidd, Grady Spring, John Miller, Gene Powell, John Augustine, Dall Cooke. Or is it Dal with one *l*? In this gentle quiet just before dawn, the ice machines humming and Eleanor's bolt cutters snipping—the quiet before a small army of vehicles full of hopeful anglers descends upon the marina—the men discuss the spelling of one of their brethren's names for a good couple of minutes. "I think it's two *l*s, isn't it?" "The newspaper spelled it D-a-i-l." "I been calling him Daryl for fifteen years." Doesn't seem to matter, overly. He's one of them and that's what counts, a captain who has spent much of a lifetime learning the secret spots of the Rappahannock River and the Chesapeake Bay, taking charter parties hunting for croaker and spot, rockfish and trout, filling coolers with fish, helping out the rookies, laughing at their jokes and watching over them like weathered preachers shepherding their flock.

Captain Buddy Muse has been at it for about thirty years. His father was a fisherman and oysterman on the Rappahannock, and though employment took him north to Pennsylvania for thirty-two years, he never let the river go. He retired and came back home, starting his charter business in a thirty-four-foot deadrise out of Robinsons Creek. In 1977 he hired Paul S. Green in Deltaville, Virginia, to build him *Ginger II*, forty-three feet of hard-working Bay sweetness. He can carry up to twenty-one passengers on her, though after he hits sixteen he has to take on a mate. Every year the Coast Guard inspects her equipment; every two years Muse hauls her so they can go over her inch by inch. Muse is obviously proud of her; despite her workboat calling, she is immaculately scrubbed and tidy. Not many more being built like her, he says, shaking his head with regret at a dying tradition. He holds

a Coast Guard fifty-ton master's license, is past president of the Virginia Charter Boats Association, chairman of the board of deacons at his church (Macedonian Baptist in Center Cross, Virginia) and is a member of the gospel choir Zion Knights for whom he sings and plays guitar—which, in addition to fishing, he has done all his life.

He sits at the helm station just behind the boat's small cabin, dressed as if he's going to casual day at the office: leather deck shoes, blue jeans, a striped shirt and undershirt tucked in neatly. A cell phone is clipped to his belt. His office is similarly businesslike—the wheel at center with throttles to its right, controls for the anchor windlass, the anchor line running next to him on a sheave (pulley) so he can fine-tune it with his hand. Above the wheel, a fish-finder, GPS, VHF radio, compass. As *Ginger II* pushes into the early light, Buddy puts on a pair of glasses, consults a small notebook, punches in some numbers on the GPS and removes his glasses again. Time to find some fish.

This is not as easy as it sounds. There's a knowing to it, and all the GPS coordinates in the world can't bring fish into the boat. By listening to the dock talk and chatter on the VHF, Muse already has ruled out heading into the Bay today. No croaker biting out there. He powers upriver to his first couple of choices, searching for swatches of hard bottom he has reconnoitered before. He can get extremely close with the GPS. But should he drift or anchor? And if he anchors, will the boat lay where he wants it to, or will the current or breeze pull her off the hard bottom? And once he has weighed all these variables, will the fish show up? At first, it doesn't seem so. Muse anchors *Ginger II* and watches carefully as his party works their lines. Lena gets the first hit. Muse walks aft to help her de-hook the unfortunate fish. "Thank you, Captain," she says, dropping the first of many croakers foolish enough to toy with her into her cooler and slapping it shut with one foot. "Now you guys can start anytime you want, don't let me stop you."

"Women's luck," one of the men grumbles. "No such thing," says Lena, flicking her line overboard and taking a pull on her Budweiser. "It's skill. It's skill. It's called *finesse*. Oh, it's so hard to be humble."

Muse smiles under his hat, takes his seat at the helm and resumes his

Photograph courtesy of James Mills Scottish Factor Store

watching, a toothpick poking out the side of his mouth. This is what he will do most of the day—watch quietly and help where needed. "Most of my parties call me the fussin' captain because I see you do something wrong, I'll tell you," he says. "Because I like to see people catch fish."

After a few hours of hunting for a busy chunk of bottom, Muse settles on a spot that's productive today—in this case, in about fifty-four feet of water just off Carter Creek near a cluster of other boats. It's not the way he likes it. "I like going off by myself," he says. But the fish are behaving oddly, scattered and spotty, and this is the best place he's found so far. The reels are spinning steadily, and coolers are slowly filling. Muse suspects the fish are traveling rather than schooling, which explains why the action comes and goes in waves. But he can't know for sure. "I'm gonna tell you the truth, I don't know," he says. "They have tails and fins and you never know about a fish."

He must know a little. He's booked nearly every day but Sunday and his parties come from as far as Philadelphia. "We each have our own clientele. Most of my parties are repeaters." He pulls out his daybook, which is scribbled with entries. "The man I have today will come again in May, twice in June, once in July, twice in August and twice in September. I like it that way because I don't worry about getting a deposit. If anything happens and his group can't make it, he'll call in plenty of time for me to get another party."

It's an honorable way of doing business that appeals to Muse, same as throwing back undersized fish or not crowding another captain if the fishing is hot and heavy in one place. A captain has to be firm but polite, savvy but not pushy. And he should enjoy people and love his work. "You get people from all walks of life," he says. "I've never had any problems with my parties." The feisty banter, which has, like the fish, ebbed and flowed all day aboard *Ginger II*, has kept him laughing, but now it's midafternoon. Time to go. Tomorrow's first light will come soon enough. Once again, Buddy Muse fires up the diesel to get his party moving. "All good days must come to an end," he tells them. He watches them pull their lines, and then turns *Ginger II* toward home. ■

CHESAPEAKE BAY GATEWAYS NETWORK

James Mills
Scottish Factor Store

With its bucolic but convenient locale on the Rappahannock River, the town of Urbanna was established around 1706 by Virginia's colonial legislature at Jamestown as part of an effort to develop centralized commercial locations for colonial trade. In 1763, an enterprising Scottish merchant, or "factor," named James Mills erected a two-story, Flemish-bond brick building on a hill overlooking what was then called Prettyman's Rolling Road—Cross Street today. Now known as the Old Tobacco Warehouse, the store is one of only two structures remaining in the United States where tobacco growers could trade their crops directly for imported European goods.

Visitors can enjoy the store's lovely grounds under large, old shade trees, just a few paces from the Urbanna waterfront. Several other colonial structures are nearby as well, including the Customs House across the street (now a private home) and the Gressit House up a narrow driveway on Cross Street. Built between 1740 and 1750, this house is reputed to have been William Clark's last stop before he departed to join Meriwether Lewis on their historic westward trek.

Window on the Chesapeake

THE WATERMAN'S DAUGHTERS

Beneath the sharp glow of bare light bulbs and the soft gurgle of river water pouring through PVC pipes, Catherine Via pulls a light blue gardening glove onto one hand and peers into a long, shallow tub of water where hundreds of peeler crabs scuttle and fuss. It's early. It'll be hours before the sun even thinks about rising. But it's May in Urbanna, Virginia, and the first soft crab run of spring is in full flood. Sleep is something Catherine can do later—winter, maybe. The crabs aren't waiting.

She works her way through a maze of sixteen shallow, eight-by-four-foot wooden tubs called floats, deftly and gently culling the green peelers (which will shed their shells in four to five days) from the ripe peelers (two days to shedding), keeping an eye on the busters (those in the process of shedding) and the soft crabs (those who've just shed their shells). She makes sure the soft crabs stay in the water for about five hours—no more and little less—before she lifts them out once and for all and takes them to the refrigerator truck that serves as a walk-in cooler. She places them in a waxed cardboard box, depending on their size (whale, jumbo, prime and hotel prime), where they will wait to go to market and land on tables from Washington, D.C., to Philadelphia. Chesapeake Bay soft shells, soft as cotton, sweet as butter.

Sometime about dawn, her little sister, Beatrice Taylor, will be along to head out onto the Rappahannock River and spend the morning pulling her pots where the "jimmies" (mature male blue crabs) have lured the peeling females. On board, she'll cull the keepers from the rest, then zoom them back to the crabhouse to place them in the floats, where Sissy, as she calls Catherine, will watch over them. Both women are grandmothers with the wrinkles to prove it, and though they're thirteen years apart, they could almost be twins. Their eyes smile the same quick way, their short hair is wavy and thick, their faces tanned, their laughter ringing in harmony.

Beatrice Taylor (left) and Catherine Via

"It all goes back to Daddy," says Beatrice. "Course, we've been doing it ever since we were little girls, catching a soft crab or two."

"The movie only cost thirty-five cent, and if you took a dime you could get a drink and popcorn," Catherine adds. "So we didn't have to catch a whole lot."

Catherine and Beatrice are Urbanna fixtures, a pure delight simply to listen to, their constant banter a wellspring of stories about the river, the town, family, and catching crabs, past and present. For instance:

Catherine: "She's always been in the boat. I can't even run a boat."

Beatrice: "Well, you can, but you just couldn't get it started. Now they got keys for that."

Most days in spring, if you wander down to the waterfront you can find them in or near the small, tidy gray building with white trim, marigolds in window boxes and petunias peeking from hanging baskets. This is the retail end of Payne's Crab House, which also serves as an office and, during Urbanna's annual Oyster Festival in November, a kitchen that turns out thousands of crabs to hungry visitors. The business end of Payne's is a few steps away, hard by the water under a flat tin roof, where Catherine tends the crab floats and Beatrice ties up her boats and stacks her pots when they're not working. Linking the office and the docks is a kind of outdoor living room. There's a picnic table with a pot of impatiens centered upon it, some lawn chairs, a sink, a hanging pot of begonias, all under a green corrugated plastic roof. Come here on a late spring morning or a summer evening, pull up a chair, and you will hear some stories. "We solve the problems of the world, right here," says Beatrice. "The Crab House is the central thing, and that's the way it was when Daddy was living. We had sofas, a chair—anybody wanted to change furniture they'd bring us down their old furniture. It was always a social place, people come and talk and look at the water. Even the little kids—first place they want to go is the Crab House. 'Let's go to the Crab House, Nana!' We start 'em early here."

If a waterman's blood flows like a river, carrying the hopes and dreams and bone-cracking hard work of generations, blessed with sunrises and riven with storms, then Catherine and Beatrice can travel their own stream back to the low-lying islands of the Chesapeake's Eastern Shore. Their grandfather, Henry Dize, came from Smith Island in Maryland and saw his bride to be, Rebecca, one day while he was on Tangier in Virginia. "He came over to Tangier to court 'er, and over there they gave him the name Lovin' Henry, 'cause they said he must love her a whole lot to come all the way over to see her!" Catherine laughs out loud when she tells this story while she leans over and slaps you gently on the knee for emphasis. Henry and Rebecca took in young Avary Payne when his mother died, and Henry passed on to Avary the ways of the water. Even today, the women speak of their grandmother with open awe. "There was *nothin'* that woman couldn't do," Beatrice says.

Eventually, the whole family moved to Urbanna, where Avary Payne ended up running his own crab house, and his daughters learned everything there is to know about how and why blue crabs shed their shells to grow bigger, how to catch them when they do it, how to clean them and dredge them ever so lightly through flour mixed with Old Bay, then pan fry them in butter. When Avary died in 1977, the sisters took over their father's business (the old Crab House is gone, although the new one stands in the same location). "He was seventy-two," Catherine says. "He had a massive heart attack right out in the river. He died doing what he loved best." Beatrice smiles. "He was always proud of us, but I think he'd definitely be proud that we are carrying on his work, *hard* work. Sometimes when I'm out there fishing my pots I feel like he's right there with me."

These days, Beatrice fishes about 120 pots, six days a week. "She was at two hundred, though, when she was feisty," Catherine teases. During the spring, the two women work almost nonstop for weeks, resting only when the rush slows, then gearing up when it starts again. In a recent year, the two sisters shipped about 19,000 soft crabs to the wholesale market—and that doesn't include local retail and walk-ins. The whole family pitches in to help: Dale, Beatrice's husband, keeps the plumbing running in the floats; James, Catherine's husband, does all the carpentry; and it's not unusual to find a few of Catherine's four sons—three of whom are in the same business—delivering crabs, power-washing pots or helping out in some other way. ("This is what got in the boys' blood too," she says. "They graduated from college and two of them were schoolteachers, but it was like being confined, you know, being in that building.") Along with minding the floats, which James helps her with as well, Catherine is in charge of packing and shipping the crabs, lining up customers, "running to the phone every whip-stitch. But it's not hard, physical work like [Beatrice] is doing. I get started at three o' clock in the mornin'. So I go home at one." She'll come back later, of course, to check the floats—every four or five hours, every day. At seventy-four, Catherine admits she gets tired. "I'm gettin' too old for it now, I know, but I'll do it as long as I can. This is the last of the waterman's heritage."

Beatrice gets on the water at 5 a.m., and spends about eight hours tending her pots before returning with her catch. She used to go out earlier, but state regulations have set 5 a.m. as the earliest, and this year the state has also restricted the soft crab's length for the first time—three inches for peelers, three-and-a-half for soft crabs. Neither woman minds, although Catherine still believes that "Mother Nature and the good Lord have more to do with it than the VMRC (Virginia Marine Resources Commission) will *ever* have to do with it."

"I'm for anything that's going to help the crab situation," Beatrice says. "It's not only this year you want to work. It's five years from now and ten years from now."

In her spare time, Beatrice, who's sixty-one, is now in her third two-year term as Urbanna's vice mayor. It's a job she takes extremely seriously and infuses with the enormous love she and her sister feel for this place, which, like so many other Bay towns, is tip-toeing its way through the mine fields of development, population pressures and changing economies. "There are not many places left like this," she says. "I think there's a spirit in this town that has been passed to us from generations back, and we have to care for that and pass it on. Urbanna is a special place. It's not just a spot on the map."

It's not something you need to be told, sitting by the water at Payne's Crab House, listening to the river of these women's lives flowing like song. ■

Photograph courtesy of Starke Jett

The Watermen's Museum, Yorktown, VA

The Watermen's Museum

The waterman's story is told at many places around the Bay. Among these is the Watermen's Museum on the banks of the York River in historic Yorktown. The museum was established in 1981 as a tribute to those who have worked southern Bay waters since the 1600s. Its intimate collection of photographs, tools, boats, letters, charts and other artifacts was contributed by area "watermen families," and captures the essence of a rapidly vanishing way of life. Adjacent to the Museum is a pier where visitors can board the *Yorktown Lady* for a cruise enriched by narrated descriptions of area history and natural features.

For almost as long as it has been standing, the lighthouse at New Point Comfort has had to worry about falling over. Back in 1801, this spot—then on the tip of a 100-acre island marking the northern edge of Mobjack Bay—seemed like a sure enough bet. Clay beneath the sand seemed solid. Two salt ponds protected it on either side, and trees and bushes nearby held the land fast. A scow could deliver building materials and supplies on sheltered water to within 150 yards of the light. Yet by 1814, only ten years after the lighthouse's construction, the Chesapeake was licking at its doorstep like a hungry dog and has been ever since. The water does not care that this lighthouse is the third oldest still standing on the Bay and among the ten oldest in the nation. The nor'easters that shred the Bay in winter could care less that Elzy Burroughs went bankrupt even as he finished the stout tower, still standing as testament to his masonry skill. The hurricanes don't remember that British soldiers sacked this light in the War of 1812, that Confederates wrecked it again in hopes that Union ships might stagger aground without its steady beam, that Jerry McHenry Farley, a minister and one of the country's few African American lighthouse keepers, found it "a

Marion Gray Trusch with light-house task force member Gary Wayne Brownley

lonely and dreary place," despite his faith in God and his devotion to the steady flame of the lamps. The fitful water that has been this lighthouse's lifelong companion has also been its steady predator. Today, a wreath of rock speckled with guano and oyster shells is all that holds it off. The 100 acres, the salt ponds, the trees, the house, the well and vaults for the oil, the soldiers, the keepers—gone. All that's left are ghosts, birds and bottle-green water. And the lighthouse.

"It could tell you somethin', if it could talk," says Edward Pritchett, a waterman who has lived all his life in its shadow and believes he is related to Elzy Burroughs on his mother's side. "Oh, it could."

It stands sixty-three feet tall and is shaped like an octagon, wide and thick-walled at the bottom and growing more slender as it rises. It's made of the same Virginia sandstone quarried for the White House, but in some places, where time and weather have worn off the whitewash, the rock is sinuously striped with the yellows, browns and coppers of desert canyons. Staring up the stone spiral staircase leading to the lantern room is like gazing into the graceful internal spiral of a chambered nautilus. The fourth-order Fresnel lens that beamed light up and down the Chesapeake is gone, but the wind still hums past the brick and iron lantern room and the deck and railing surrounding it. In 1963, the Coast Guard extinguished New Point Comfort's light and demoted the lighthouse to a day marker, the same pedestrian status bestowed upon pressure-treated poles jammed into the mud and topped with a green or red triangle and a number.

As lighthouses go, New Point Comfort is really rather plain, lacking the quaint architecture of the Bay's screwpiles like Thomas Point or the loftiness of the Cape Hatteras tower. Its beauty lies in its simplicity, and its stoicism. For 200 years, it's always been there, and for the people who live nearby, who have grown up within its sight, that's enough. "The one thing that everyone agrees on in Mathews County is that lighthouse," says Marion Gray Trusch. "Everyone loves it." Marion Gray's great-grandfather Wesley Ripley (the family called him Big Pa), was a sea captain and tended the light from 1881 to

1883. "My father as a young man used to stay in the house with him and help him keep the light, and my father would say that was the most beautiful thing on a moonlit night, to go up there at night and light that light and see the Chesapeake Bay where it meets the Mobjack Bay. He talked so much about it I almost felt like I was up there with him, and that's why it's important to me."

Marion Gray, as everyone calls her, was a schoolteacher, but in another life she could have been a lightkeeper. In a way, she is now. Every day, the eighty-two-year-old makes the pilgrimage to the lighthouse overlook, a small walkway located in ninety-five acres of Nature Conservancy preserve. She just likes to see it there, a tall white candle in the distance. And there came a time when she decided she'd had just about enough of seeing that light dark every single night. The lighthouse needed a lamp, and she was going to put one there. "It was not hard to do," she says. In relative droves for this neck of the woods, people stepped up to help. They formed the Lighthouse Lantern Committee. Her niece Ida Trusch, a graphic designer who camped at the lighthouse as a youngster and holds the memory like the magic of a first kiss, designed a poster of the light. Marion Gray and others sold it everywhere they could to raise some money—about $3,000—so the county wouldn't have to fork over one single cent for the project. A helpful young Coast Guardsman worked hard to get permission to install a light that would not be used for navigation. The editor at the *Gloucester-Mathews Gazette-Journal* gave the project lots of prominent ink. Edward Pritchett ferried volunteers to and from the lighthouse on his crab skiff. Local cabinet maker Gary Wayne Brownley worked with the Coast Guard to study the light's history and now, along with his brother, Stephen, and Edward Pritchett, helps maintain the lantern, which was lit on December 12, 1999. It's a simple set-up, powered with a solar panel and generator. "You can see it a right good ways," says Pritchett. "And it's just nice to look at."

It was an honorable and worthy step, but the next move is a leap far more expensive and uncertain, and it's probably little consolation that people were hemming and hawing about it as early as 1814: How to keep the lighthouse standing and well-maintained? "A lot of work needs to be done here. I mean it's a helluva challenge," says Earl Soles Jr., of nearby Cobbs Creek, chairman of the New Point Comfort Lighthouse Preservation Task Force, a committee of the Mathews County Historic Society. To learn as much as possible about the light, the task force commissioned a lighthouse historian to research its past, and her report reveals clearly the light's long battles with erosion, vandalism and weather. Autumn gales of 1815 brought water to the light's foundation, and Elzy Burroughs suggested various ways to protect it—from building a piling-and-fill seawall to moving the entire building. (At the time, they chose the former). That's not too far from what the task force is considering now, says Soles. Among the options are adding more granite to the stone already in place, building jetties that with luck would encourage sand to accumulate around it, or even building a berm and using dredge spoil to create a new island around the lighthouse. The task force was also seeking engineering studies to learn more about the lighthouse's foundation, since no one knows for sure what's under there. Its members want to figure out how best to restore the lighthouse and perhaps make it more accessible to visitors. They are seeking the advice and thoughts of the community. And of course, the group has to find money. Bags of it. "It is," Soles says, "a huge community effort." One that everyone hopes the lighthouse can wait for just a while longer. It has, after all, endured this much. ▪

**Mathews Blueways
Water Trails**

New Point Comfort lighthouse punctuates one of the loveliest waterscapes in Virginia. Perfect for exploring by canoe or kayak, five interconnected water trails, the Mathews Blueways, offer more than ninety miles of idyllic passage into the heart of the tidal ecosystem on the western shore of the Chesapeake Bay. Mathews County is a small rural county sporting more than 200 miles of shoreline and dotted with quaint fishing villages and historic wharves where ferries and steamboats once called. The area is laced with three tidal rivers and fifty navigable creeks with sixteen boat-launching sites. In addition to excellent seasonal fishing and paddling, Blueways water trails—including the Piankatank River, East River, Winter and Horn Harbors, Gwynn's Island, and the New Point Comfort Trail—are a birder's delight, with frequent sightings of species ranging from great blue herons to the once-endangered osprey.

THE WATER AND WALTER COLES

Walter Coles Burroughs leans against the rattling engine box, takes a careful sip of scalding coffee and looks across the flat green water he knows will always be there. But for the water, everything changes, God knows, even down here at the distant tip of Mathews County, Virginia, where the land doesn't so much end as flatten and soften, until it finally swoons before the inevitability of water. Where ten houses and two families can make a town. Where the finger of land probing Dyers Creek known as John's Point—named for Walter Coles's grandfather—has been home to Burroughses and Hudginses for as long as anyone can remember. Roots this deep can hold some comfort. Walter Coles (that's what everyone calls him, given name and middle) was born here, raised here, schooled here. He married here, raised a family and has worked his pound nets here. He will, he reckons, die right here, too. But anyone who lives on this tenuous fragment

of earth knows a storm tide can still heave a casket right out of the churchyard, and a strong wind can lay a loblolly right down. After all, Walter Coles will point out, it was a Burroughs who built the sandstone lighthouse out there on New Point Comfort back in 1804, and when he did the sand dunes running out to the light were tall enough to nearly eclipse the beam. Miles and miles of them, solid waves of sand, fuzzy with live oaks. Gone, now. Just the lighthouse left standing on a scrap of rock, alone. The Lord put that land there, boy, and He can take it away. Just like He did Walter Coles's daughter, Thelma Lynn, when she was just twenty-five. Leukemia. Just like He did his wife, Dot. Alzheimer's. Walter Coles leans against the engine box, sips his coffee and, for what seems like the hundredth time this day, tries not to cry. Eventually, he sighs and fixes his eyes at the flat green water that spreads out before him like rippled glass. It's an uncommonly peaceful day for November, warm and calm. "I reckon I'm selfish or somethin' cause you know what?" Walter Coles says, shedding his jacket. "If I could screw a clamp on it or somethin' I'd do it right now. This suits me." Tomorrow the Bay might be mean as a junkyard dog. Or not. But the water is always there.

Walter Coles is seventy-four and he has been a pound net fisherman nearly his whole life. His blue eyes are clear, his hair is white, his hands are at once rough and gentle, and if you ask him, he'll say he's old. Forgetful. His daddy was a pound net fisherman before him, his uncle too. Mathews County, in fact, was the first place on the Chesapeake a pound net was ever set well enough to catch anything worth noticing. A fellow named Snediker came down from Long Island and in 1875 set a pound net off New Point. When the locals saw how much he hauled in, they cut down his nets and ran him out. Before long, though, they started setting nets themselves. Walter Coles recalls nets so thick off New Point, you had to snake your way through them. Boats coming into the wharf at Sand Bank wallowed with fish. That wharf's gone too, now, nothing but a bunch of pilings sticking up from the bottom like a row of rotten teeth. Walter Coles and his son Ronald are among the very few left working nets in Virginia. It takes a solid crew of men to work a pound net, and steady labor is harder to come by every day. So are fish, and the market to sell them. Friend of his down in Gloucester (the next county to the south) who had a big rig—bigger even than Walter Coles's—quit this year, went to work at the oil refinery instead. And once they're gone, he says, they're gone.

Walter Coles's rig is a wooden, fifty-one-foot, Bay-built round-stern named *Ginnie*—named for the wife of the friend from whom he bought her. She's thirty-six years old and wears every year twice. But she's tough, and the sharp slope of her sheer up to the bow gives her the cheeky look of a woman who knows her age and how she got there. Her little cabin house has a stove and a couple bunks, but mostly she's one long, open cockpit that serves as work area and fish hold. A stubby telephone-pole mast stands just behind the cabin house and carries a gaff pole used for lifting. Tagging along behind her as she chugs across the sandy, scalloped flats outside Dyers Creek is an open boat thirty-five feet long, tethered to *Ginnie* with a single thick line. Some places on the Bay, Walter Coles says, they call this boat a skiff, but around here it's known as a fishing bat, probably short for batteau (or bateau).

Today Walter Coles and Ronald have five crew: Joe, Wayne, Jim-Bob, Kenneth and Calvin. At the height of the season, if the fish are running hard, they'll take as many as nine. Kenneth is well traveled—he was a captain on a trawler in Maine for many years and drove tugboats up and down the coast for a time. Joe is a young man and so is Jim-Bob. Walter Coles will admit Jim-Bob can get aggravated at times, but he's a good fisherman and he has three young mouths to feed. Walter Coles doesn't miss a chance to tell Jim-Bob he's a millionaire, his children love him the way they do. You can be a poor man, he says, but if you have a loving family and live a moral life, you're plenty rich. Jim-Bob's too young to know it yet. A man has to live a long while to find out.

On this warm day, Walter Coles is wearing a baseball cap, a thick sweatshirt and a set of fatigue-green, Helly Hansen bib overalls. When he left the kitchen this morning, he walked into the garage in stocking feet and stepped into the tall white rubber work boots he wears fair weather or foul. Pound netting is wet, slippery work, and he'll wear these boots till he walks back into the garage, steps out of them, and heads back into his quiet house where the wide green

water won't be able to turn his thoughts from Dot. Walter Coles Burroughs and Dorothy Grey Hudgins were sweethearts three years before they married on October 21, 1945, four days before he went into the Army. She was seventeen, he eighteen. Fifty-six years we've been married, he says. She's gone two years, and he still talks about her as if she's back in the kitchen, frying up some chicken for his lunch, waiting for him to come home. They had a few cross words, Walter Coles admits. Man and a woman raise five kids, you can bet they'll have a word or two now and then. But they stuck together. Shoulder to shoulder. Raised their family best they could.

It takes about twenty minutes to reach the first of Walter Coles's two pound nets, where Ronald, who raced ahead in his little Boston Whaler, is already tied up and lounging in the sun. The net's hedging, or leader, stretches like a fence across the Bay for 175 feet or so, lashed to a series of stakes pounded into the bottom. The leader ends in a wide bay formed by two stakelines cupping each side like a pair of hands. The bay ends in the pound head, a forty-two-foot-square corral made of stakes and seine net that hangs thirty feet to the bottom and attaches to a net floor. On the surface, it looks pretty simple. Underwater, it's a complex network of ropes, pulleys, chains and thimbles that can loosen or snug the net tight, raise it up and lower it back down. It's a devastatingly efficient system: a fish (or turtle, or shark, or stingray—even a cormorant or loon) that's swimming along hits the leader. He turns and follows it, trying to get around the end. But the end leads him to the bay, which eventually leads him through a narrow funnel of net into the pound head. And there he waits for Walter Coles.

Ginnie rumbles up to one side of the head and Kenneth and Calvin tie her off. Walter Coles kills the engine, and the limpid stillness of the morning rings in the silence. Not even a wave to kiss *Ginnie*'s hull. Some of the men light up smokes, some lean back and close their eyes. They wait. "Water clear some," Walter Coles says. "You see any, boys? Huh?"

"Water's clear as I've seen it, I b'lieve, in my life," answers Kenneth. They peer into the green, looking for tide, for fish, for whatever they might see. You never know what the Bay will serve up. Sometimes the nets are full of cormorants. Been awhile since they caught a big shark, Walter Coles says, many years. Pretty quiet today, and the water peaceful.

Walter Coles will tell you—you can't hold a tide. Top of your nets get thick with four-eyed jellies and sea nettles and grass and the tide will just mash the whole damn thing right down. You can't hold a tide. Back in '33, the tide came calling. He was six years old then, and when he woke that morning, his momma told him not to bother getting out of bed—it was blowing and raining, and his daddy wasn't going fishing today. Walter Coles looked out the window of his family's big white house on the point named after his grand-daddy and saw the Bay prowling up his front yard like a feral dog, ravenous but wary, creeping forward and back, side to side, but never, ever quite stopping. One minute you'd look and swear it had held up or maybe even was backing off some, the next it would be lapping the porch. Before long, it was up the steps and through the door, brown as Ovaltine. They didn't name

storms back then, and why should they? Nightmares don't have names. It was the storm that sliced New Point in half, casting the light-house loose from its shore like a fisherman gone overboard in the dark. It drove the water high as a man's throat down by the post office and blew birds up the Bay no one had ever seen before. That tide washed pound nets

clear down to Cape Henry and beached eight-ton workboats half a mile inland. You can't hold a tide, especially one driven by storm. And so when the gray tide of Alzheimer's started creeping across Dot's brain, Walter Coles at least knew where he stood.

"Ronald!" he calls across the water to his son basking in the Boston Whaler. "Y'all got no tide, eh? Drop seine end and leave it, straight up and down." That's what Walter Coles is waiting for. Slack water. Only then can his crew move the bat into position across the opening to the bay, and then draw up the funnel to close off any exit for the fish. Then they start hauling the net slowly into the bat, ropes wrapped across their butts and the backs of their thighs so they can lean into the pulling, make levers of themselves. Below, the still water of the pound's head starts to stir, at first flickering jets of silver flashing just beneath the surface, then, as the bat draws deeper into the head and the net comes up tighter and tighter, a panicked, fluttering pile of fish crowding the net's southern end. The men are mostly silent. Now and then one will groan at the weight as they hand-over-hand the net into the bat. Beside them, the thousands of fish writhe in the ever-tightening pocket of net as the bat moves closer and closer to *Ginnie* across the pound head. Walter Coles, who has been watching from *Ginnie's* aft deck, cranks up the engine

and uses the gaff to lower a long metal pole with a net on one end that resembles a bathtub-sized basketball net with its bottom pinched shut. Ronald grabs the net and the line controlling its bottom. Like scooping ice cream, the men push the net into the squirming fish until they're spilling out the top. Walter Coles kicks the gear to raise the pole, holding onto the far end, and maneuvering it over the center of *Ginnie's* cockpit. Then Ronald yanks the line, the bottom of the scoop net opens, and a flood of fish crashes into the hold, where they slap the deck and each other, frantic at first, then slower and slower. The men repeat the scooping until the net is empty and the cockpit is a writhing, frothing sea of alewives and sea trout, rockfish, and flounder, croaker and even a couple of crabs. A single eel swims and snakes over the whole pile. When Walter Coles kills the engine, the perfect silence resumes its dominion over the morning, broken only by the wet slapping of the dying fish. Without saying much, the men lower the funnel again, move the bat out of the head and reset the net.

Most of this catch will go to crabbers for bait. Not much else in here, except for what rockfish they can tag and sell for eating, and that's a minority—most of them get thrown overboard as one of the men wades knee-deep through the fish, flinging keepers into one corner and tossing the rest. It's the end of the season, and the nets are slim pickings. And even thinking about rockfish gets Walter Coles a little worked up. He's an advisor on sea trout to the Atlantic Coast Marine Fisheries Commission, and more than once he's stood and spoken his mind about what he considers dangerous meddling in the natural order of things. Rockfish, for example. When he was younger, the pounds never caught rockfish. Since the government started saying a man could only take so many (and for many years none at all), the Bay's rockfish stocks have rebounded. And now the crabs are in trouble, and you know what a rockfish loves to eat. Crabs. At least that's how Walter Coles sees it. Nature has her own ways, he says. Man has no right to meddle.

Walter Coles fires up *Ginnie*'s engine and the men cast off to head to the second net just a bit farther offshore, and repeat the ritual they practice just about every day from April through November, the ritual which marks the rhythm of Walter Coles's life. Depends on the tide, when they go fishing. Sometimes they get to enjoy this warm sun, other days it's a hell-fired blast furnace out here. Some days it's midnight when they head out, and the south-westerly blowing up from the Atlantic is like a warm, wet kiss, the stars rain down over their heads and the restless water makes it tough to work the nets. But it's something to see, anyway. Harder the wind blows, more the birds fly. Seagulls and pelicans, they'll hang up there in the breeze, wingtips balanced on the darkness, waiting for daylight and their world of wind to calm down. That's what you have to do sometimes when the wind gets up, just wait it out.

The birds are following *Ginnie* as she heads back in on a falling tide, and right there, Walter Coles says, is a mystery. When he was growing up, pelicans never came up the Bay. Several years ago, he and Ronald set a little net off York Spit Lighthouse, and when they put it overboard in June, three pelicans came and sat on that net. They stayed all season. Now pelicans are predictable as sweet corn in summer. Walter Coles laughs. "There's a saying I got. If we could make as much paper today or tomorrow that they already have, that much more, double it, it wouldn't write down what we don't know. We think we're so smart, but that wouldn't write down what we don't know."

You can be a young man to understand this, but it takes an old man to believe it. A man who has seen the air so clear some nights that lights twenty miles south are bright as headlights coming down your driveway. Seen fish vanish from the nets for decades and then reappear like they were never gone. Seen one storm rearrange the geography of whole lives easy as a schoolteacher moving chairs around. Seen a mother, a father, a daughter and a wife laid down in the ground. There's a comfort in knowing you can't explain it, or predict it, or even stop it. It's out of one man's hands. Walter Coles will fish his pound nets, ponder the mysteries he finds there, argue with fisheries managers, tie up *Ginnie* and let the younger men spend the hours it will take to cull and box the fish for market. He'll walk across the oyster shell lot from the dock to his house on the low flat land where Burroughses and Hudginses have lived since anyone can remember, step out of his boots in the garage, go inside and eat some chicken and maybe a biscuit. He'll wait for the burden of night and then another morning, to head out again where the water is wide, and will always be there. ▪

SHAD

It's a little like magic, the way Henry Langston can set 200 feet of five-inch-mesh seine net to drift on the incoming tide, net so fine it looks like it'll tangle if you so much as breathe on it too hard. He sits quietly in the back of his olive-green aluminum skiff, clips an orange, Clorox-bottle sized float to one end of the net's top line, tosses it overboard and then starts quickly, methodically flinging out net, which is piled carefully in a plastic trash can. Every so often he grabs the tiller of his four-horsepower outboard, adjusting his course. Every twelve feet or so a small orange cork attached to the top line pops out, and pretty soon the little floats bob in a long half-moon across the still water of the Pamunkey River, off a little scrap of bog known as Doc's Island Bar. Langston can't say why it's called that. Nor can he know for sure whether he will catch some spawning females, or roe shad, and some males, which he calls bucks, or just come up with nets tangled in alewives, which he calls mud shad. Nor can he offer any real explanation for how he manages to set all this net so cleanly, so quickly. Practice, maybe. "Well, I've been doin' it a long time," he says. "I've been fishing out here a long time. We didn't have motors. I used to pull with one oar, my first cousin pulled the other." His granddaddy would set the net. "We pulled the boat, and he put the net in," he says. It was spring then too, the low, wild riverbanks laced with white dogwood and wild azalea. They would wait until just before twilight to head out fishing, because that's when the roe shad like to come upstream, back up the river of their birth. Henry Langston can't say why evening is the best time, either. It just is. Always has been.

He's taken off his Ray Bans and his eyes are a hazel brown, the irises rimmed in a startling turquoise. His baseball cap is sweat-stained, and his long-sleeved shirt is tucked neatly into green corduroys, which disappear into a pair of thigh-high, mud-brown waders. He is seventy-three years old, and his wiry frame is strong, his hands and face nearly unlined. His quietude suits this murmuring, low-country stretch of river where shad have always run in the early spring twilight, where Pamunkey Indian boys learned from their granddaddies how to set a gossamer net to drift, and that they'd better not play with a snapping turtle or it might grab them and not let go until the next thunderstorm.

After setting a second net, Langston chugs back to the first one. He is eyeing the floats, which tell their own stories. "See how this cork is heavy?" He points to a float that is just slightly deeper than its neighbors—a barely perceptible difference to an unknowing eye. "It's holding. It's not riding the waves. It's got weight on it." That means something is pulling it down, and depending on how the float moves—with quick little jerks or longer, smoother tugs—it's likely a mud shad or the real thing—a buck or roe shad. "Sometimes they'll fool me," Langston says, "but usually if it's calm I can tell." He cuts the outboard. Sculling carefully alongside the net, the middle

of his oar wrapped in frayed duct tape where it rubs against the boat's gunwale, he stops at the float and slowly pulls up the net. Glistening like a silvery rainbow, a roe shad emerges from the muddy water, hopelessly snagged in the net. Langston lifts her gently, cradling her body with both hands and sliding the net off of her. "That's the lady," he says, running his thumb and forefinger along her stomach, kneading and squeezing. "But she is not ready." He shakes his head and lets her slip over the side.

This is how it will go, well into the evening as the tide starts pulling the nets and the boat faster upstream, and the sun sinks behind thunderheads growing purple in the northwest sky. They won't amount to anything this day, after all. Langston will quietly watch the floats, check the nets and wait to find a spawning roe shad. He'll squeeze the eggs from her—maybe a thousand of them—into a small white bucket, then find a buck and squeeze a few drops of sperm into the bucket too. "Then we stir it, let it set two minutes, then add some river water into it. It sets about an hour. Those eggs swell up and you run your hand in there and they feel like BB shot or something." After he's gathered as many eggs as he can, he'll pull his nets and skim back to the dock beneath the sycamore trees next to the shad hatchery, where Pamunkey Indians like Henry Langston have been serving as shad midwives since 1918.

"We've been fishing all our lives, and the river was a way of life," says

Warren Cook, vice chief of the Pamunkey Tribal Government and shad hatchery administrator, a job Langston held for six years. "We decided we wanted to help put shad back in the river. We're the oldest shad hatchery in the United States."

The Pamunkey trace their ancestry in what is now Virginia back some 10,000 years. When Captain John Smith sailed up the James River and helped established Jamestown in 1607, the Pamunkey were the most powerful of the tribes comprising the vast Powhatan Confederacy. The new settlers eventually imposed their will upon the natives, and a 1677 treaty that the Pamunkey negotiated with the colonists lays it out pretty clearly, stating the natives could "enjoy their wanted conveniences of oystering, fishing and gathering tuccahoe, curtenemons, wildoats, rushes, puckone or anything else for their natural support, not useful to the English . . . Always provided they first repaire to some publiques majestrate of good repute and inform him of their number and business." The rest, as they say, is history. The Pamunkey of today keep their own tribal council and maintain a reservation of about 1,200 acres, some 500 of which are wetlands. About seventy-five residents live on the reservation, which is also home to the purported gravesite of the great Chief Powhatan and a terrific museum describing Pamunkey history.

Shad were always a part of that history. The Pamunkey used the fish for food, for trade, for money. But even in the early twentieth century, they were attuned enough to the vagaries of the river and its species to know that hatching baby shad in a controlled environment and giving them a head start in a river full of predators could help the population grow. Their first hatchery had an 800-gallon holding tank, a gas-powered motor and hatching jars. During the 1950s, the hatchery started using "tidal boxes"—wooden boxes with mesh floors that could be tied off a dock in the river itself and preclude the need for pumps and holding tanks. In 1989, a new hatchery with tanks and pumps was built, and it grew steadily until 1998, when a huge upgrade—using a Chesapeake Bay Program grant and matching state money—brought the hatchery to its present form: fifteen 250-gallon fiberglass tanks, twenty-four hatching jars, a maze of white PVC pipes, flanges and valves connecting them all to holding tanks filled with river water. In 2001, the hatchery released about 3.2 million fry into the river, and some years it has managed up to 5 million. Shad fry from this hatchery helped start successful restoration efforts on the Susquehanna and James rivers.

For five to six weeks each spring, the hatchery buzzes with frantic activity as fishermen like Langston bring in the fertilized eggs. They're placed in tall plastic cylinders—three-gallon hatching jars that can hold up to 100,000 eggs—where they swirl slowly as pumped water constantly moves around them. If left still, they'll die. Dead eggs, which look a lot like the tapioca you find in pudding, are siphoned off constantly. When the live ones start hatching, the jars are hung next to the 250-gallon tanks swirling with tea-colored river water. At this stage, the fry are barely visible, the size of a needle's eye, transparent with two black flecks for eyes. As they're born, the current moves them up the hatching jar, over its lip and into the big tank. Here, after three days (they're born with a three-day food supply conveniently hanging in a pouch beneath their throats) they grow and swim and eat brine shrimp which a timer squirts into the tanks every five minutes, twenty-four hours a day. After about fifteen days, the tiny fish are tagged—a precise process of introducing a soup of oxytetracycline and water into the tanks. The chemical penetrates the fish's ear bone, which enlarges in concentric circles like the rings of a tree. That ring, distinctive to this hatchery, will show up clearly under a microscope, and through this tagging scientists can track the fish. After being tagged, the fry are released straight into the river at night—the better to avoid predators, Langston says. They're only about the size of a sharp pencil tip at the outset of their long, mysterious journey downriver to the Bay and then to open ocean, hopefully to return here in a few years to spawn.

Out on the river, the day is waning. Meadows of tuckahoe sprout along the marshy shoreline of the reservation, where ospreys hunch in oak trees fuzzy with the first brilliant green of spring. Langston points to the little creek where, when he was a youngster, he would launch his boat on the high ground and paddle out to the river. The floor of his boat is flecked with fish scales, like silvery petals. He has always fished, and even though it's harder these days—age is catching up to him, he says—he probably always will. "Go ahead," he says as he gently slides a roe shad back into the immutable dark river. "Go ahead." ▪

**Pamunkey
Indian Reservation**

Today the Pamunkey tribal lands encompass about 1,200 acres along the Pamunkey River in King William County east of Richmond, Virginia. Laced with streams meandering through pillowy, forest-fringed wetlands, the resident Pamunkey community of thirty-four families nestles on land awash with Chesapeake history. Entering the reservation one passes a monument dedicated to the Powhatan princess Pocahontas, and tribal lore holds that a nearby, modest mound of earth may hold the mortal remains of her father, the great Indian ruler Powhatan. The nearby village of White House was the home of Martha Custis Washington; later the area witnessed its share of Civil War strife.

Like other native peoples of the region, the Pamunkeys hunted, trapped and reaped the Bay's bounty of fish and shellfish, and a reservation museum tells the tribe's enduring story. The Pamunkeys also developed a strong cultural tradition of pottery making, using local clay and calcinated, freshwater mussel shells as raw materials. The ancient potter's craft became the basis of the Pottery School organized on the reservation in the 1930s. Pottery-making still thrives there, with today's Pamunkey potters making both painted and glazed objects as well as the tribe's traditional mottled gray-and-black, stone-polished vessels.

Window on the Chesapeake

Deep in the woods of the Dragon Run, mystery and beauty entwine. For some forty miles near the headwaters of Virginia's Piankatank River, the Dragon's

A FRIEND OF DRAGON RUN

swamps, streams and marshes embrace a wilderness unparalleled on the Chesapeake. Gossamer bells dangle from the pink stems of fetterbush, and the buttonbush bloom like tiny supernovas, translucent spears of light shooting from their bright white centers. Bald cypress trees loom from the water, their massive trunks as wide as eight feet. Mistletoe clumps in the treetops, and turks cap lilies flame like a thousand orange suns against the rich green of the wetland forest. Otters slide through the dark water, beavers build, ospreys and eagles soar and keen above. So removed from reality

is this place, so magical and dense, you might not be surprised to find an elf flitting among the shadbush. Or perhaps a sprite tucked into a kayak, her bright blue eyes quick, her camera and sense of wonder at the ready.

Teta Kain is not a photographer by profession. Nor does she get paid much, if anything, for pursuing any of her other varied passions as an environmentalist, birder, moth and butterfly watcher, writer, publisher, public speaker, kayak tour leader, amateur herpetologist and botanist, sky-diver. But this is a woman who, given the option, will run—not walk—down the stairs to her office in pursuit of some thought or another. A woman who decided upon turning sixty-two to use her Social Security check to buy kayaks and to pay to jump out of perfectly good airplanes. Repeatedly. ("I'm kind of a wimp because I had a hip replacement and they don't want me to jump solo," she says. "When you jump tandem, of course, you come down on a nice soft little instructor.")

Now sixty-five, her list of volunteer work for groups including the Friends of Dragon Run, the Virginia Society of Ornithology and the Chesapeake Bay National Estuarine Reserve is three times as long as most CEOs' resumes. Petite and compact, she bubbles with energy and excitement, salting it with a quintessentially yankee bluntness delivered in the flattest of Maine accents. The license plate on her red Chevy Blazer—the one with the red kayak strapped to the roof—reads "PQULYA." Around the York River near Gloucester, Virginia, where she lives in a creekside house brushed by pines that hum and sigh in the wind, she's a bit of an exotic species herself.

She came to the Bay—and to her naturalist's passions—a roundabout way, starting in "Bah Hahbah, Maine, and that's as good as I can say it," leaving there when she was seventeen to eventually become an Air Force nurse. "I was going to stay in there forever and become a general and run the world," she says," but a little guy from Arkansas swept me off my feet. I've had him in training now for forty years, and he's beginning to catch on." The man in question is her husband, Reece Kain, who through much of the 1970s was stationed in Nebraska, North Dakota and Missouri, manning Minuteman missile silos. One day in Missouri, she and Reece got into a little argument over a black-and-orange bird that flew across the road. "I said, 'That's a redstart,' which was the only bird I knew that wasn't common, and he said, 'That's not a redstart, that's a Baltimore Oriole.' I said, 'I know more about this than you do,' so I got a book, and of course he was right. It was a Baltimore Oriole. But that book had a list in the back to check off the birds you had seen, and that's what got me hooked." It was a revelation to learn, she says, "that there were people who would look at birds and not shoot 'em."

And it seems that once she started really *seeing* birds, she couldn't stop there. "When you're looking at birds, you can't help but become a conservationist because you see things changing, and sometimes not for the better," she says. "I was obsessed about putting a name to all the flora and fauna." She took up photography to document all that she was learning and seeing. When Reece was assigned to Langley Air Force Base in Virginia, Teta thought the culture shock might flatten her. "The Midwest had my heart," she says. "But immediately upon getting here, I could see the diversity of this state. Now you couldn't pry us out with a crowbah. We're here to stay."

She wasn't here long before she heard about a place called Dragon Run. "When people hear the name, they never forget it," she says. Situated in the middle of Virginia's Middle Peninsula—deep in farming and timbering country—most of the Dragon is so remote that large swaths of it are barely touched by humans. In some areas, it's a mile-long trek through rugged wilderness to reach the Dragon, and some parts of it are so narrow, a canoe can barely sandwich between the cypress knees and marshy hummocks. The land around and along it is privately owned, in many cases by families who have held the property for generations. In the mid-1980s, as residential development and industrial pressure started squeezing even the remotest Bay tributaries, a local pharmacist concerned about the Dragon's future got about thirty people together who donated enough money to purchase 203 acres. Friends of Dragon Run, of which Teta is vice president (and chief photographer), now has more than 400 members and owns about 300 acres. It is working steadily to purchase more land or convince property owners to put their land into conservation easements, and to educate them about ways to continue their businesses while having the least effect on the river and its ecosystem. And it's keeping an eye on any potential threats to a watershed that the Smithsonian Institution, in a survey of 232 areas in 12,600 square miles of the Bay region, has ranked as second in ecological significance.

This is what Teta Kain wants people to know when she takes them on kayak trips down the Dragon, or spends night after night hunched in her little kayak, prowling through the darkness listening to the owls and peepers and racoons, photographing frogs and spiders, turtles and minks, and other shy denizens of the marshy forest. Her home is decorated with beautiful color photos of the Dragon and its inhabitants, and she's quick to set up a slide projector in her office downstairs to show off more. "I'm not a real shoutin' conservationist. Never have been," she says. "Many environmentalists are very negative—you can't do this and you can't do that, and they don't give any alternatives or compromises. Well, it's obvious that none of us can have it all. If I can show them though my slides and programs that something is beautiful and worthy, then maybe I'll start a fire somewhere."

Teta gives up to forty programs a year throughout the state to yacht clubs and retirement communities, civic groups and garden clubs. She speaks on a variety of subjects close to her heart—bird feeding, nesting, bird songs, fungi, wildflowers, butterflies and moths, reptiles, amphibians, Dragon Run and even the Great Dismal Swamp. "Have projector, will travel," she laughs. "I'm a ham. I love it." She's a life member of the Virginia Society of Ornithology, having joined in 1982 and been on its board since 1983, devoting years to it in every capacity imaginable, even preparing information on every species seen on every Christmas bird count in Virginia back to 1904, serving as editor of *The Raven,* and developing an electronic index of the publication and key words from all the articles, volumes 1-70, so anyone can research them. She has conducted bird studies with the U.S. Fish and Wildlife Service and the Audubon Society, and now is a member of the North American Butterfly Association, routinely inviting gangs of people over to her house for nocturnal moth watches. She's a member of the Virginia Native Plant Society and the Virginia Herpetological Society, is serving a five-year term on the Gloucester County Wetlands Board, and let's not forget that she has conducted water quality tests from her dock on Caffee Creek every single week since November 1989 (okay, so she missed one week when she had to attend a bird meeting in Colorado).

"I live in my kayak in the summer. I do a lot of trips, especially on the Dragon to educate people about it. I am the official paddle master. I have a little Swiftie kayak, it's about ten feet, and I can tear around just like a little waterbug."

She reckons she spends about ten hours a day, seven days a week, at her various non-professions. "It's not a job," she says. "To me, I'm not working hard. I could, if I wanted to, just say the hell with it all, and that gives you a whole different perspective. For me, life is very exciting. I wake up every morning and I say, I wonder what's going to happen today?"

One thing seems certain; if Teta Kain has anything to do with it, *something* will happen. ▪

York River Water Trail

Not far from Dragon Run, the evolving York River Water Trail traverses the waterscapes of three rivers: the broad, tidal York, which empties into Chesapeake Bay, and two of the York's tributaries, the Mattaponi and the Pamunkey. The trail's approximately 120-mile length includes numerous access points and opportunities for paddlers and boaters to explore natural and historical sites ranging from the Pamunkey Indian Reservation and bucolic York River State Park to the Revolutionary War battlefield and historic village at Yorktown.

Dr. William Kelso, the man who is doing his utmost to rewrite a seminal moment in American history, is rummaging around the artifacts vault at Jamestown Rediscovery Center like a youngster rifling his toy box, intently looking for that *one, single thing.* Surrounding him are hundreds of thousands of artifacts, critical clues that are helping to reveal a more honest and accurate story of the first English settlement in America at Jamestown, Virginia, than our history textbooks have told us. But what he's looking for—a gold signet ring bearing the crest of the Strachey family—is special to him, for it is firm evidence that America was being settled even while William Shakespeare was still writing his plays. William Strachey was secretary of the Jamestown colony, and his shipwreck near Bermuda en route to Jamestown in 1609 was said to inspire "The

Tempest." If he just wanted to show the crest, all Kelso would need to do is hold out his hand; he wears a replica of the ring on his pinky. But that's not the real thing. So he rummages, opening drawers, peering into boxes, stopping here and there to hold up a tiny compass inlaid in a fragment of ivory, a piece of a woman's comb, flat squares of copper that local Native Americans wore as jewelry. Finally, a murmur of discovery. There's the ring. Even safely encased in a small plastic baggie, it's like a jolt of light across the chasm of nearly 400 years.

You might think that as director of archaeology for Jamestown Rediscovery—what some are calling the premiere archaeological dig in the nation—William Kelso would get enough excitement telling the world that his team has found sufficient evidence to rewrite history. Evidence to indicate that the generally accepted thought about Jamestown being an ill-conceived, badly staffed, greedy fiasco that resulted in little more than suffering and death has been wrong-headed and uninformed by what the archaeology could tell us. That instead, the people who came here in 1607, who struggled and suffered, died or managed to survive, left a legacy on this marshy piece of earth as the true birthplace of the United States and its representative form of government. This is heady stuff, indeed. Almost as good as what Kelso calls "the moment of discovery," when all of his research and thought and hypotheses are put to the test, and he carves a trowel into the earth, starts to shave away centuries and finds—exactly where he thought it should be—a gold signet ring, or an iron helmet or a dark swatch of dirt revealing the footprint of a long gone fort. That moment is so powerful, so truthful. "It happens and it's gone, it's a passing thing," he says. "It's an immediate connection to the past. This is as close as you can get to time travel, when you find something in situ that's 400 years old, and the last person to touch it was some colonist."

The first time Kelso stepped onto Jamestown Island he was studying for his master's degree in history at the College of William and Mary in nearby Williamsburg, Virginia. He was curious about the low-country, piney island known to be the site of the first permanent English settlement in America. The story he knew was essentially what we had all learned: In 1606, King James I granted a charter to a group of London businessmen called the Virginia Company to sail to North America, establish an English settlement in the Chesapeake Bay and find gold. Led by Captain John Smith, the settlers endured the Atlantic crossing, entered the Bay and sailed some thirty-five miles up what would become known as the James River, landing in May 1607 at a scrap of island. There they established a fort to ward off attacks from the native Algonquian of the Powhatan Confederacy, and, through indolence, incompetence or both, managed to lose most of their number to disease or famine. They never found gold; ultimately it was tobacco and timber that earned the company money. Eventually—and thanks to the intervention of the new governor, Lord De La Ware—the colony struggled along long enough to convene the first representative assembly in the New World in Jamestown Church on July 30, 1619. An Algonquian attack in 1622 killed more than 300 settlers, and soon thereafter the king revoked the company's charter, making Virginia a crown colony in 1624. Over time, the old fort disappeared, though Jamestown remained Virginia's capital until its statehouse burned in 1698 and the capital was moved to Williamsburg. By the mid-1700s, the island was little more than a bug-swept farm. Jamestown—and, largely, its significance— faded, as other settlements with aspirations loftier than financial gain (most obviously Plymouth, Massachusetts, which was settled thirteen years after Jamestown) assumed favored historical status as America's birthplace.

On that day in 1963, Kelso breathed in the salty pine air on Jamestown Island and walked among the granite monuments to Captain John Smith, the spooky remains of what's believed to be a church tower built in 1639, and the Confederate earthworks where live oaks were growing. Unlike most visitors, he was looking for what he couldn't see—the remains of that first landing of Englishmen on American soil in 1607, James Fort. Gone, he was told, no doubt washed into the river long before.

Kelso didn't buy it. But it was thirty years before he would return to Jamestown and begin to satisfy his curiosity. He studied and worked on colonial Virginia projects under Ivor Noel Hume, who trained him in historical archaeology—a way of re-examining historical sites through the prism of archaeology. An historian by training, Kelso found his imagination fired by the immediacy and purity of archaeology. "It gives a third dimension to history, and makes the story you already know on an intellectual level richer and more credible," he says. What the earth relinquishes "is untainted evidence. There are no hidden agendas or biases that you sometimes see in the written records and histories." He served as director of archaeology at Colonial Williamsburg's Carter's Grove, and while at Monticello excavated the slave quarters, helping provoke a much broader and more honest discussion of Thomas Jefferson and his plantation.

All the while, Jamestown Island lay quietly waiting. The Association for Preservation of Virginia Antiquities (APVA), founded in 1889 largely to protect Jamestown, had acquired twenty-two acres of the island. (In 1934, the National Park Service obtained the remainder, and the two maintain and operate it jointly today). In 1900, the APVA built a seawall to prevent further erosion, and

over the years various monuments were erected around the site to commemorate its significance. But that was it. Very little actual archaeology was conducted there, as the APVA was reluctant to disturb what it felt was sacred ground. The island was a time capsule simply waiting for the right person to pop the hatch and decipher its messages.

As the 400th anniversary of the 1607 Jamestown landing approached, the APVA board decided it was time to try to discover, once and for all, if James Fort could be found. In 1993, the organization hired Kelso to lead the search, and a year later, bringing all of his historical study and gut feeling to bear, he started digging in an area between the river and the church tower. Within the first day, he unearthed English pottery and clay pipe fragments dating to the 1600s. Within a few months, he and a squadron of assistants had uncovered a dark streak of soil—a trench that had held wooden palisade walls. Within a year, they had unveiled part of a circular moat, as well as another wall heading off at an angle from the first.

A corner of James Fort's footprint had been found, and within it were more than 150,000 artifacts dating from the early 1600s. From the angle provided by the corner, Kelso has been able to extrapolate where more walls should be, and preliminary digs have proven his theory. "The main fear was the Spanish coming and wiping them out, which they were going to do. It makes so much sense that the fort is here," Kelso says, his pure white hair windswept as he stands near the broad back of the river beside replica palisades that have since been pounded into the ground on top of the original wall. "It's the highest ground on the island. It's two hundred feet from the channel, hidden from incoming ships by about a half a mile." The settlers, he says, made a well-reasoned and sound strategic choice for the fort. Its location alone is evidence that they could not have been as hapless as history has portrayed them.

And there's much more to indicate the same. So far, Kelso's team has found a treasure of about 400,000 artifacts: "It's just astounding the quality and the quantity, and the stories they can tell." For example, he points to sheets of copper, and smaller squares of the material with a hole punched in a corner to create a pendant. The settlers knew the Powhatan coveted copper as jewelry, and clearly they were fabricating it to use for trade. The archaeologists have found equipment to study metallurgy, make glass and glass beads, smelt iron (including bullet molds) and work metal. "This whole idea that they came here and didn't want to work and starved to death is overstating it," he says. "People were working here." They have found few agricultural tools, but it's clear the settlers were using the river's resources for food—hooks six inches long have been found, as well as sturgeon bones and turtle shells. There is also chilling evidence of the starvation that haunted the colony— bones clearly indicating horses, cats and dogs were butchered for food. Kelso says it appears the settlers' relationship with the Powhatan was far more complex than historians have believed, and that perhaps some of the natives may have lived within the fort. For instance, Indian pottery was found inside the fort walls, as were almost 200 knife points and the shards whittled from rock to make the points. "I don't think the English were making stone tools. They had their own iron. It wasn't all an us-against-them thing." Remains of a building show how the English began to adapt to their new environs, at first using typical English wattle-and-daub mud construction, but then changing to the post-and-bark methods the Powhatan preferred.

It is, Kelso believes, only a beginning. There are dozens of graves to excavate, which can reveal more about the population of settlers: who they were, what they faced in this new place and how it changed them. "We can define what the cultures were that left Europe and learn how did they adapt and change and start becoming Americans. Everything we find has something to say about that." There are the rest of the fort's walls to find, the wells that must have been dug, the remains of an early church and statehouse to probe for clues. Plenty of chances for William Kelso to feel that jolt across time. "A lot of people would be frustrated by the anticipation, but that doesn't bother me," he says. "I've got to believe I haven't found the high point yet, because I still get excited to come here every day and go out there and look." ▪

View of the James River from "New Towne"

CHESAPEAKE BAY
GATEWAYS NETWORK

Jamestown Island

Surrounded by the soft natural beauty of Jamestown Island, a part of Colonial National Historical Park, Jamestown Rediscovery archeologists dig from April through October and the associated laboratory is open year-round.

The site's "Old Towne" section encompasses the crudest, pre-1620 settler dwellings and the recently uncovered James Fort, in addition to remains of the 1639 church tower. But this is a place of layers, and in Old Towne the strata reveal the third and fourth colonial Virginia statehouses, built in the late seventeenth century, and earthworks created by Confederate soldiers in 1861. The adjacent "New Towne" section features what is left of more substantial, post-1620 settler houses, with some reconstructed foundations. Nearby is a re-created traditional colonial glass factory where costumed interpreters create glass mugs and other objects using traditional glass-blowing methods. A Visitor Center offers interpretive maps and an orientation film.

Window on the Chesapeake

Charles Hill Carter III likes to surprise people, and he does. The heir to Shirley Plantation, the oldest colonial plantation in Virginia, wouldn't wear a cravat if one whacked him between the eyes. The eleventh generation to live within the grand rooms in this James River estate fifteen miles south of Richmond has been known to unplug telephones that irritate him and engage in what he calls "diesel therapy," noting that he can't even *hear* a cell phone while working a backhoe, let alone answer one. It is true that he will, on a cool clear morning, stop and smell the winter honeysuckle blooming next to the north porch through which, in another time, house slaves would bring the Carter family meals cooked in the kitchen, well separated from the main house. "To get a whiff of that," he says, "it's a nice thing." But he is a businessman and a farmer first and foremost, and Shirley is his family's business, his family's farm. Just so happens it is the oldest family-owned business in the United States. And while tens of thousands of tourists annually oooh and aaah over its hand-carved eighteenth-century paneling, the one-of-a-kind "flying" staircase, the Old South aura that permeates its brick walls like that sweet winter honeysuckle, it is simply home for Charles Hill Carter III, a place whose survival he has known, since he was a boy, would fall to his shoulders. He does possess wide shoulders. Good thing. "It's preserve, protect and pass on the plantation, and whether it's fixing up the

marble Hepplewhite tables in the hall or fixing the mined uplands or building wetlands or fixing a hollow brick wall, it's all restoration," he says, standing beneath a 300-year-old willow oak gracing the front yard, as a setting spring sun gilds the two-story porch facing the James river. "It's not the life of the rich and famous. This place busts a lot of reality."

The 50,000 tourists a year who visit Shirley, though, are not interested in this reality. They are looking for the past, and the past, through the prism of Shirley, is all about the rich, the famous and the culture that enabled them to be both. It started in 1613, when Thomas West, third Baron De La Warre, was granted 8,000 acres on the James. He named the estate West and Sherley Hundred—the Sherley for his wife, Lady Cessayle Sherley. After West died, Colonel Edward Hill in 1638 obtained some of Sherley Hundred, what is now the site of the plantation. Jamestown, about thirty miles downriver, had been settled in 1607, and with tobacco becoming Virginia's version of Spanish gold, landowners like Hill were establishing vast properties to support it, moving upriver as they went. Eventually, the shores of the James between Jamestown and Richmond would be lined with plantations whose grand and elegant names matched their masters' social and economic ambitions—Evelynton, Berkeley, Belle Air, Westover.

Sherley Hundred's fortunes were to take a fateful turn when Hill's only son died, and his sister Elizabeth was left with the property. It was a pickle. She couldn't marry just anyone—because whomever she married would be inheriting her accidental birthright. She chose prudently, though, when she accepted the hand of John Carter, Secretary of Virginia Affairs, and married him in 1723. Carter was the son of Robert "King" Carter, a member of the House of Burgesses and one of the most powerful men in Virginia with more than forty plantations numbering better than 330,000 acres. (When he died, his holdings included 10,000 pounds of sterling and 734 slaves.) The marriage ensured that Shirley, as it came to be known, would have deep pockets and political clout to secure its success.

John Carter began building the present home the year he married Elizabeth Hill, but they didn't move in until 1736. The features that today make Shirley a national architectural treasure were there from the outset, beginning with the carved black walnut A-square staircase that rises three stories with no visible means of support (two wrought iron straps hidden within the structure cradle the stairs and are anchored in the brick outer wall and the second landing). There also are the enclosed, Queen Anne forecourt—the only one from its time period still intact in the country—framed by a two-story brick kitchen; a two-story laundry that also served as a schoolhouse; a granary with a thirty-five-foot-deep icehouse in which ice harvested in winter could stay solid well into summer; and a tool barn (other buildings include a dovecote and stables). And there is the three-and-one-half-foot pineapple topping the mansard roof, a symbol of hospitality for which Shirley would become known. The bricks, glass for the windows and fasteners were all fabricated on site, and the timber was local.

Elizabeth and John's son, Charles Carter, took charge of Shirley in 1770, a year after his mother died (his father had died in 1742). During the Revolution, Shirley was a supply center for the Continental Army and was used as a listening post between the British and Lafayette's Army. In 1793, Charles Carter's daughter Ann Hill Carter married Revolutionary War General Henry "Light Horse Harry" Lee III in the parlor at Shirley. Their youngest son, Robert E. Lee, would spend a great deal of time as a youngster at Shirley, receiving much of his early education at the school in the laundry house, and would go on to command the Confederate Army.

One reason Shirley remains so intact is that it survived the Civil War relatively unscathed, while many of its neighbors were ravaged. In July 1862, after the Battle of Malvern Hill nearby, hundreds of wounded Union troops arrived by ship at Shirley's wharves and used the plantation's outbuildings as hospitals. Hill and Mary Carter helped care for the wounded. "You can't watch that kind of suffering," Carter says, "whether they're your enemy or not." Later that year, Hill obtained a federal safeguard from Union General George McClellan, and in 1864 Union troops even stood guard around the plantation to divert marauding Yankees. Charles Carter also suspects Shirley was spared because it was, after all, the birthplace of Robert E. Lee's mother.

Today, the tenth and eleventh generations of Carters still live in the home in its upper floors, leaving the ground floor open to tourists. The kitchen is now in the basement, and the heating and ventilation systems use the same cast-iron ductwork and artistic circular brass vents that Hill Carter installed in the 1830s. "I have 50,000 tourists a year in my living room and I attribute all my character flaws to that," jokes Charles Carter, forty, who with his brother Randy and sister Harriet operates the 700-acre plantation. "I was born and raised here and I was the oldest son, and I knew from the git-go that this would be my responsibility."

Talk to Charles Carter and you get the distinct feeling that his love affair with his home place is like most passionate relationships—adoration and devotion coupled with self-sacrifice and struggle. For Shirley, he has given up much of his privacy and, to some degree, autonomy over his own destiny. But the idea of failing her is unthinkable. He's a barrel-chested giant of a man with hands like ham hocks and forearms to match. His resemblance to his forefathers, whose gold-framed oil portraits hang throughout the house, is astonishing. His tanned face is framed with thick brown hair, and he smiles a lot. He looks like a farmer, and at heart he is, although Shirley has demanded much more of him than that.

Shirley's history, however remarkable, is not enough to support it. When his father, who is now eighty-two, inherited the plantation in the 1950s, Carter says, "it was in tough shape. Deferred maintenance was going to bring the place down." Tourism alone would not be enough to finance the upkeep and restoration of such a place, even with 50,000 tourists a year paying about $10 to visit. "If we cut our rates we could probably run a lot more people through here, but I don't want to do that. I want to find the least number of people to stress the place the least." Farming wouldn't support it either; only about 250 acres of the land is planted. "Diversity," he says, "is the thing."

For example, during the late 1960s, about 280 acres of Shirley's land was mined for sand and gravel. Today, Carter is using the mined areas as disposal sites for hundreds of thousand of cubic yards of clean dredge material from the construction of the new Woodrow Wilson Bridge in

**Chippokes Plantation
State Park**

The James River and its winding
tributary creeks drew aspiring
planter-entrepreneurs almost
from the moment Europeans
set foot in what would become
Virginia. In 1619, Captain
William Powell was granted
550 acres on Chippokes Creek,
across the river and about
thirty miles downstream of
Jamestown Island in what is
now Surry County, Virginia.
Later the plantation grew to its
present size of 1,403 acres, and
later still, in 1854, its gracious
brick mansion house—the river
side stuccoed and painted
white as a landmark for vessels
on the James—was built.
History lives here, for Chippokes
is one of the oldest working
farms in the nation. A state
park since 1967, the plantation
is operated jointly by the
Virginia Department of
Conservation and Recreation
and the Chippokes Plantation
Farm Foundation. Its treasures
include lovely formal gardens
around the mansion as well as
the usual state park offerings
such as camping, cabins, and
picnic facilities. A farm and
forestry museum on the grounds
displays rare farm implements,
many forged by hand, and
other artifacts that bear witness
to the arduous life and
unflagging innovation
demanded of early
agricultural communities.

Alexandria, Virginia. He is being paid, essentially, to return his land to its original elevation, which also fits nicely with his overall goal to restore Shirley's landscape to its 18th-century splendor.

Charles Carter makes no bones about his willingness to do whatever he believes it takes to help Shirley, no matter how radical it sounds. "In the family business I describe my role as special projects," he says. "If it's crazy, it's my kind of project. The gritty reality is that it is good to accept mud from the Wilson Bridge project because it will restore the land." He rents a building on the plantation's pier to a fledgling boat builder, and is working with tour boat operators in Richmond to bring visitors to Shirley via the James, docking at the pier. He is also working with the Alliance for the Chesapeake Bay to create a submerged aquatic vegetation nursery and 20 acres of wetlands on the cove's backside.

Meantime, the house and outbuildings need constant, careful upkeep. It is all a delicate balancing act. Carter admits that living in a house that's better than 260 years old—a house that must maintain its historical integrity—can be "damned inconvenient at times." But he also knows how careful he must be to concede to Shirley's past. "You can start making a lot of little compromises here and wake up in ten years and you will have lost something you can never get back." In the end, it's a fairly simple thing that guides him in his stewardship—he loves this place, the way the sun sets across the river and butters the porches with late-day light, the way the walls breathe with history, the way the winter honeysuckle smells outside the north porch door. And that's really not so surprising, at all. ■

FUTURE UNCERTAIN

The dining room table in the home of William Jennings Hargis Jr. is, in a word, a mess. Largely this is his fault. His is a roving, inquisitive, peripatetic mind, and it has manifested itself all over the table, where books are stacked on the lace tablecloth, charts of the Chesapeake Bay sag against the candlesticks, and, because it's close to Easter, a Winnie the Pooh Egg Decorating Day coloring book nudges the flower centerpiece. "That's not my coloring book," Hargis notes, in case one thought it could be. "We have eleven grandchildren." He shovels a space clear and immediately starts blanketing it with blue-shaded sheets of paper which depict, in various formats, oyster reefs of the Chesapeake Bay. On one, a black-and-white photograph shows Point of Shoals Lighthouse at low tide in 1885, a mound of oyster

reef curling around one of its legs and threading off into the distance. That same reef is graphically represented on a computer-generated, three-dimensional image with a red line denoting the top of the reef in the early 1870s—a hump of shell fully exposed at low tide, snaking more than three kilometers across the James River. Another computer-generated chart shows all that's left by the 1940s—a single red smudge. More clearly than any words, these graphic images reveal the destruction of the Bay's oysters and its reefs. "To my way of thinking," Hargis says, "these are part of the background of whatever you are going to say about the restoration of the oyster reef system."

Whatever you are going to say about oysters in the Bay, the work of Bill Hargis will probably be wrapped within it. He has studied the Chesapeake's most famous bivalve for fifty years. But in a way, those years of research are the minor part of his contribution. Though oyster research brought him back to his Virginia home after a brief hiatus at school in Florida, it is the development of the Virginia Institute of Marine Science (VIMS) of which Hargis is most proud. Under his tenure as director from 1959 to 1981, Hargis grew a small aquatic biology master's degree program at the College of William and Mary into an internationally recognized center for estuarine and coastal studies, where today fifty-six professors and more than 100 graduate students conduct the time-consuming, crucial research to help scientists, regulators, legislators and citizens better understand how to solve the Chesapeake's myriad health problems. "What I hoped to create," he says, "was an institution that could study all the physical, chemical and biological characteristics of the Chesapeake Bay, find out what's going on and make recommendations. I helped build awareness. I think it will be of long-term value to the Bay and the future of the country. When I say, 'I,' you have to filter it through the ego, but I built this place. So if you call that being satisfied, then yes, I'm satisfied."

At eighty years of age, Hargis continues as emeritus professor of marine science at VIMS, now one of five graduate schools of the College of William and Mary. He keeps an office in what he calls "Geriatric Hall" (Marshall House, where many of the emeritus professors work) and it's not unusual to see him marching about the forty-acre campus at Gloucester Point on the York River. In fact, he looks something like a lord in his domain. "Everybody looks at me as kind of being avuncular, the old guy," he says. "That's okay with me as long as you do what I want you to do." He is irreverent, blunt and tends to poke fun at most things, the better to see them for what they truly are.

He has spent his eighty years like a man on fire—undergraduate degrees from the University of Richmond, doctorate from Florida State, a decade as an Army Air Force pilot, founding dean of the College of William and Mary's School of Marine Science, presidential appointee as chairman of the National Advisory Committee on Oceans and Atmosphere, co-founder of the Chesapeake Bay Council, chairman of the Chesapeake Research Consortium, chairman of a joint U.S.-Soviet committee to study the world's oceans, stewardship or involvement in dozens of committees, task forces, councils and boards—nearly all related to coastal, estuarine or ocean studies and research. He has traveled far and wide, but the Bay is his home—his mother was from Tangier Island, his father from the mountains of Virginia—and his profound love for its history, its cultures and its creatures is what has driven much of his career. "I don't know if it's the same kind of love you feel for your spouse and your children," he says. "But it's palpable, the love for the Bay."

His career, and the development of VIMS, took off largely because of oysters. They were dying in droves in the Delaware Bay in the late 1950s, and on the Chesapeake, where oysters had been an essential element of the economy and the culture since well before Colonial times, scientists, legislators and watermen all watched fearfully for the same disaster. It wasn't long in coming. For thousands of years oysters played a huge role in keeping the Bay healthy. And they became the Bay's canary in the coal mine; their demise has foretold of the Bay's complex health problems, from lack of oxygen to nutrient overload, over-development and sedimentation. The need to study and understand those complex relationships was what spurred the growth of VIMS. "It became apparent that oceanography had to be brought into the estuaries," Hargis says, "and while there were outfits like Woods Hole [Oceanographic Institute] studying the deep ocean, nobody was looking closely at the Bay until really after World War II."

The Chesapeake Bay's once astounding oyster reefs developed some 7,000 years ago. Early explorers remarked on their size and abundance, and it wasn't long before they were heavily harvested. By the mid to late 1800s, annual harvests reached 100 million pounds. It could not last. Oysters are slow-growing animals that filter feed by siphoning water; just by the act of eating they clean the water of sediment, oxygen-robbing algae and nutrients. One adult oyster can filter up to fifty gallons of water a day, and scientists say that at one time, the Bay's oysters could filter the entire Bay in three days. Today it would take the remaining oysters a year.

But oysters also depend on the reef to grow; without something hard on which to anchor themselves, where they will grow for the rest of their lives, oyster larvae cannot survive. For thousands of years, the Bay's reefs provided that habitat, as well as supported dozens of other species. It took only a few hundred years of unabated harvesting to demolish the reef system. Living oysters were harvested, but so was old shell—the vital strata of the oyster reef. It was scraped away by tongs and dredges and mined to be used for construction, soil enhancement, building roads and even landfills. According to Hargis, between 1920 and 1944 alone, Maryland and Virginia reported producing more than 2.7 tons of shell byproducts. Hargis's new three-dimensional charts show that even by the late 1800s, the damage to the Bay's once extensive oyster reefs was monumental; reefs once substantial enough to break the water's surface at low tide were shrinking, and within five decades would be reduced to mud. Without the hard strata on which to set their spat and grow, oysters by the late 1800s were already in a downward spiral. When, in the 1950s, the diseases MSX and Dermo were introduced into an already weakened oyster population, the results were total devastation. "Disease contributed, but it was just topping it off," Hargis says. "The reef system was destroyed by overharvesting and removal of shell. As long as the habitat was intact, oysters did quite well."

Today, oyster harvests barely reach 100,000 pounds annually, and despite state and local efforts to revive the population and rebuild reefs, it is a painfully slow process whose outcome remains uncertain. "I don't think we're making the headway we need to—by 'we' I mean environmentalists and research scientists—against the forces of destruction," Hargis says. "It's one of those things you can't stop."

It's a pessimistic view, but one to which Hargis may be entitled; a person doesn't spend decades watching research and science wrestle with politics, government and special interests without getting a little gloomy about the possibilities for real change. But it's not enough to stop Bill Hargis from continuing his passionate study of this place he loves so well. Nor, even after half a century, to keep him from continuing to throw down the gauntlet on its behalf. ▪

Gloucester Point and Gloucester Point Beach

Perched at the tip of Gloucester Point where the York River opens into Chesapeake Bay, the VIMS campus is surrounded by the momentous history and cultural traditions of the southern Chesapeake region. Still visible in nearby Tyndall's Point Park are remnants of earthworks that shielded both Union and Confederate soldiers from musket fire. The fortifications, in turn, like VIMS itself, overlie colonial Gloucestertown, a riverside depot where Virginia tobacco was stored before being shipped to Europe.

Tucked in near the base of the George W. Coleman bridge, which connects Gloucester Point with historic Yorktown Battlefield, is Gloucester Point Beach, a local haven for picnickers, anglers and watersports enthusiasts.

SLOW HAND

The hands of a wooden-boat builder are a study in contradiction. Gnarled and thick, rough as a mountain range, they are surprisingly delicate as they place a frame just so. They are patient as they fair a corner of deckhouse, and gentle as the fingers run down a smooth length of hull, barely brushing the wood. As if they're feeling for a pulse.

Jimmy Drewery's hands are like this. They've built traditional Chesapeake Bay workboats for decades, faired acres of decks and hulls and bent out miles of chine. His most recent boat is a fifty-foot Carolina-style sportfisherman he and a small crew, with right-hand man Bernard West, built as a working exhibition at The Mariners' Museum in Newport News, Virginia. In all his sixty-two years, it's the first boat he's ever built from actual drawings rather than what's known as rack of eye—essentially building a boat bottom to type just by eyeballing it. "This boat's got a wild, crazy hull," Drewery says. "You've got to loft it to get it right."

That much seems true. Typical of the Carolina style, the boat's bow is flared like a contortionist to divert ocean waves and spray, and its transom is one long, graceful arc. Its hull sides aft are curved as well, a rather old-fashioned design characteristic known as tumblehome. But what appears rather radical on the surface is remarkably traditional underneath. Drewery built this boat as he has dozens of others, starting with its keel, bending its chine [the spine-like intersection where a boat's sides meet on the underside], building its bottom upside down and then flipping it to work his way up the hull sides and finally to the deck and cabin house. The cross-planked hull bottom is pure Chesapeake deadrise, with white cedar planks stretching from the keel outward to the chine, rather than fore and aft. Drewery opted for this generations-old method, he says, "because we knew how to do it, and because I know it's the strongest construction."

Drewery is a soft-spoken, graceful man. In the shop where dusty work shirts drape the walls and wood shavings scatter like sweet-smelling confetti, he wears khaki pants and a formal (if dusty) oxford shirt. A Virginia native, his southernness comes through in a certain graciousness, and in the cadence and accent of his words—*idea* sounds like *idear*, *want* sounds like *whunt*. He turned to the water after school, working as a commercial fisherman. In 1979 he decided to build himself a new boat—not that this was particularly extraordinary. For generations, it was common for watermen to build boats in their spare time. "We usually always built them in a backyard, covered 'em up with any type of containment we could and go from there," he says.

Invariably, these boats were built rack of eye—without plans. "You've an idea of what you want," he says. "When we start a boat, we call it bending the chine." The hull's bottom is built upside down, starting with laying the keel. Drewery then puts wooden spreaders (usually three of them) fore to aft across the boat's beam. Then he literally bends the chine, stretching a long, laminated

piece of wood from the bow stem to the stern plank, fastening it to the ends of the spreaders, eyeballing the curve all the way. "You bend it, you look at it, and if it looks like you want it to look you keep it. If it doesn't, you take it apart and adjust it till it fits what your eye wants to see." What your eye wants to see, he says, is based largely on what you want the boat to do. "If you want a boat that can run in shallow water, you want a bottom that's relatively flat. If you want a boat that runs in the Bay, you give it a little more V, so the boat can take the water and not beat itself to death. You can do all kinds of things with the chine. You can lift it way up to give it a really sharp entry [as he did the sportfisherman], and that gives you some speed. I've always tried to compromise, tried to stay in the middle of performance and stability." Bending out the sportfisherman took a day, he says.

While many watermen may have built a boat or two in their yards over their careers, few have found the art in it that Jimmy Drewery has. After his first boat—a forty-two-footer built of Virginia spruce—he didn't look back. He didn't exactly hang out a shingle; he just kept building boats, here, there and everywhere, he says, using the methods and ways he learned from the men who'd done it generations before him. "I worked that boat till somebody wanted it worse'n I did, then I built another one," he says. "I enjoy doing it. I dunno. It's just somethin' that's fun to do." Eventually Drewery started building boats for The Mariners' Museum as working exhibits. He helped well-known local builder Billy Moore build the first *Mariner*, a thirty-two-foot deadrise on display at the museum. He also built *Mariner III* (with help from school students) and *Mariner IV* (now privately owned in Norfolk). And he helped Ron Pack build the fifty-two-foot *Mariner V*, which Pack keeps at his inn and marina, Smithfield Station, on the Pagan River. "When we build a deadrise, every frame in that boat is different, except for maybe four frames aft," Drewery says. "When we build a deadrise, we just shape it the way we want."

Drewery's works-in-progress at the museum show, start to finish, the design and construction methods of a traditional Bay deadrise, a term which, for him, takes on many meanings. In its most common definition, deadrise is the angle formed from the turn of a boat's keel to the chine or turn of the bilge. A flat-bottomed boat has very little deadrise angle; a deep-V boat has a large deadrise angle. But in Drewery's boatbuilding lexicon, "deadrise," while still a function of geometry, is also linked to a specific area of a Bay boat's geography. "I have to show you," he says, and we walk into an early spring drizzle over to a nearby open shed where *Mariner* is on display. Drewery folds his long frame into a squat near the boat's bow and places his hands on one point. "You're fitting the bottom board into the chine at this point, and the point where you leave the chine square-edged is the step. The step is where deadrise begins. The deadrise starts where the bottom and sides constitute a 45-degree angle, and that's basically where you have to start steaming or chopping planks to make them fit. Wherever that happens, that's where we start planking the deadrise."

Jimmy Drewery would not be so pretentious to say that in building these boats and passing on this knowledge he is preserving an art form, or even a way of life. He knows it's true, though. With the Bay's fishing industry in decline, people just aren't building boats like they used to. "Everybody's using what they've got or getting out of it." But there's still enough of a demand to keep Drewery busy—and building boats is still a steadier business than fishing from them. Besides, he enjoys the work.

Beyond the boat shed doors, a restless spring sky opens enough for a glint of sunlight, then closes in on itself again. In the ringing silence following a table saw's whine, birdsong sweetens the air. Drewery's next project is a more traditional hull, a forty-two-foot deadrise similar to *Mariner V*. He points to a pile of lumber and some boxes in the corner. "There it is," he says, "motor and all." He puts his rough hand gently upon it, feeling for a pulse he knows will soon be there. ▦

MONITOR MAN

Curtiss E. Peterson is, at heart, a gearhead, and this is good, for he has one hell of an engine to wrestle. Most of it is a rusty mess, it's pretty much in pieces and any spare parts he needs he'll have to fabricate himself—or cajole, bribe or beg someone else into doing it. There's also the small matter of its age—140 years old—and the fact that it's been sitting 240 feet down in the Atlantic Ocean for the last 139 of those years. Oh yes, it's also a priceless artifact from the Civil War, so simply whacking it together with no regard for historical accuracy is not an option. And so, all this begs the question: Can he rebuild it? Curtiss—Curt on the little plastic tag that identifies him as chief conservator of The Mariners' Museum—slides his eyes into a sly grin, though the rest of his expression stays perfectly poker. "Yes," he says, and even his voice seems to smile at the prospect of this historic heap of iron and copper taking shape once again. "*Yes.*"

The engine in question belongs to the *USS Monitor*, the Union ironclad that famously duked it out to a stalemate with the Confederate ship *CSS Virginia* in Hampton Roads on March 9, 1862. A stalemate may not seem like much, but when you consider that the *Virginia* had been laying waste to the blockading Union fleet, which was utterly unable to penetrate her iron sides, fighting her to a draw was no small matter. In fact, the battle changed naval history, signaling the looming obsolescence of wooden sailing warships. With her nine-foot-high, armor-plated turret that could rotate in any direction, the *Monitor* could aim and fire her guns without having to move her own position—a revolutionary development in naval warfare still in use today. She was also the first completely steam-powered U.S. warship. Her innovative 400-horsepower engine, which operated on a horizontal axis, could rotate the propeller shaft at a 90° angle from the cylinders, lowering its entire profile so it could be squeezed into the ship's low freeboard. She couldn't sail worth a damn, though—in fact, on her stormy maiden voyage from Long Island to the Chesapeake she shipped so much water through her turret that she almost foundered, and her crew nearly suffocated when her ventilation system failed. It was a prophetic trip. Nine months later off Cape Hatteras, under tow to North Carolina, another storm finally took the *Monitor*, four of her officers, and sixteen crew to the bottom. There she rested, slowly rusting and transmogrifying into a reef, until she was discovered in 1973 by Duke University scientists.

Curtiss Peterson dips his hands into a clear liquid in a blue plastic tub and gently retrieves what looks like a series of small metal discs side by side. He thumbs away the dripping chemical bath like a father wiping soap suds from a child's cheek, and suddenly something is visible, beautifully scripted numbers encircling each disc. He dips them back into the bath and washes his hands, then picks up the round metal face plate of an engine register. "Monitor," is written in filigreed Victorian script arcing under the top curve of the plate, "1862," along the bottom. In the middle are rectangular spaces where the digits on those small metal discs would slowly click over, showing the engineer how many hours were on the ship's coal-fired steam engine. How did that man do his job? Why did he do things the way he did? Did he run his hands across the face of this register, perhaps wipe off the coal dust and smoke residue with his sleeve? These are the sorts of questions Peterson ponders as he delves deeper into the guts of the ship's engine and the ship itself. "I'm interested in the history of technology, how it works, what it does," he says. "This is so complex, there's so much going on. I'm hoping to get a picture of how this worked. I want to see the system in it. I want to get some idea of what was going on and why was it going on. What had to happen to make the *Monitor* go? What did these guys do and why did they do it that way?" He looks for answers as he slowly, meticulously dismantles this machine, recording everything, trying to determine what went where and how it worked. "You can't conserve a forty-ton engine anymore than you can eat an elephant," he says. "But you can take a bite. And that's what I'm doing."

By appearance alone, Curtiss Peterson is a most unlikely elephant-eater. He looks like an absent-minded professor who maybe sings barbershop on weekends. One shoelace insists upon untying itself, and the renegade tail of his striped shirt keeps trying (with frequent success) to escape his pants. His moustache is bushy, as are his brows. But it's the hands that reveal the elephant eater; they're rough and grimy—beyond the redemption of the pumice hand cleaner in his shop. And on his belt is another clue: a Gerber multitool— a Swiss Army knife on steroids. He has a quick and subtle sense of humor and a free-range mind that chews enthusiastically on information and mystery, like a dog gnawing a gristly bone. An anthropologist with a degree in chemistry, he has more than thirty years in the field of maritime archaeological conservation, working on artifacts from Spanish wrecks off the Florida coast and the *HMS DeBraak* in the Delaware Bay, among others. In his job as the museum's chief conservator, he is the proverbial kid in the candy store; the museum and its grounds are stuffed with intriguing nautical artifacts awaiting his attentions—engines, machines, submarines, priceless navigational instruments, you name it.

But "big salty metal," as he calls it, is Curtiss Peterson's specialty. And the *Monitor* artifacts—retrieved from the ocean floor by the National Oceanic and Atmospheric Administration and the Navy—are his present priority, the museum's most ambitious conservation project to date. Most of them are bathing silently in huge blue construction dumpsters in the museum's back lot, right next to Peterson's remote office—a small trailer which he calls "the skybox." Inside, he apologizes for the mess; he's in the process of remodeling to make more room for conservation work. Still, the slightly suppressed chaos of his desk and its environs seem to tell the tale; the man's mind is always moving onto something far more pressing (not to mention interesting) than pedestrian house cleaning. A trash can is spilling over with styrofoam coffee cups, a pair of black wellies sit beneath the desk, awaiting wet work in the tanks; papers and boxes are all over the place. On one wall are engineer's drawings of a *Monitor*-type rudder and propeller, as well as drawings of the ship's fifteen-ton condenser—all of which are among the big salty metal objects awaiting his study and attention in tanks outside.

And there, where pieces of the *Monitor* rest in chemically controlled baths to slowly remove corrosive salts and the encrustation that had turned the ship into a reef, it's perfectly clear what Peterson is up against—a gigantic, three-dimensional puzzle. The pieces are here: the engine room ladder; parts of a bilge strainer; a boiler; an ornate wheel that changed the engine's valve timing so it could go into reverse; yards of pipe; countless flanges; a steam header; hull plates with rivet holes rusted as big as half-dollars; the propeller and its shaft, attached to a chunk of the transom; little copper cups called oilers that were mounted on each corner of the twenty-four-foot-long engine. While some portions of the machinery are still intact, many are scattered and disassembled, their relationships to one another broken. As Peterson conserves each piece, he must figure out how they worked with each other. Then he has to rebuild everything that made the *Monitor* run—from the front, at the engine register, to the back, at the propeller.

Along the way, he wants to learn about people, and the ship's technology can educate him. "I want to know what an operational engineer needed to know just to get on the job," he says. "These were clever, smart, happy and scared people like everyone else, and they did a good job. They identified and solved problems in their context, and these are some of their solutions." Already, he has learned a great deal. For instance, divers found hundreds of intact glass whale-oil lamp chimneys. He suspects they broke a lot on the ship, so the crew had stashed backups in places or containers where they would not break. Peterson carefully lifts one from a box, and holds it next

The Mariners' Museum

Established in 1930 by philanthropist Archer M. Huntington and his sculptress wife Anna Hyatt Huntington, the Mariners' Museum is renowned as one of the finest maritime history museums in the world. In addition to permanent exhibitions on Chesapeake Bay history and culture, the Age of Exploration, and U.S. naval history—including its evolving *Monitor* Center—the Mariners' houses more than 35,000 maritime artifacts including carved figureheads, scrimshaw, decorative arts, and a dazzling collection of ship models. Other collections include 600,000 rare and antique photographs and, in the Research Library, an array of rare antique atlases and maps. Several times each year Museum curators mount special exhibitions; recent ones have explored the worlds of pirates, seafaring women, the saga of the doomed *Titanic*, and the transatlantic slave trade. A separate building houses the International Small Craft Center, home to dozens of indigenous watercraft from cultures around the world. All this maritime lore is plunked in the middle of a 550-acre park that sports miles of wooded walking trails and the 167-acre Lake Maury. On a pretty day, you can rent a rowboat or spend an idyllic afternoon picnicking and watching the park's resident wildlife—everything from red-cockaded woodpeckers to sliding turtles that plop off their logs if you venture too close.

to a conserved, gimballed lamp holder, its base beautifully ornate. "The *Monitor* was dark," he says. "And we're finding a lot of pumps." Which meant she was wet. Dark and dank. She was loaded with coal; the ocean floor is littered with about sixty tons of it. "This was an industrial plant, a factory, with belts, levers. She had a pressurized fire room—neat stuff. It was really hot in there, and it stank all the time because the pressure would leak fumes into the main areas."

It can be a rather schizophrenic life, being conservator of the *Monitor* artifacts. On the one hand, it's all big-picture. It takes months to rid the metal of the salts that want to eat it, days and days of meticulous measuring of the solutions in the tanks and tracking the amount of salts being emitted. The ship's anchor, a solid—and therefore relatively easy—chunk of iron weighing 1,800 pounds took sixteen months to conserve. "When is it finished and how can you tell?" Peterson asks. "We make a lot of assumptions and the tricky part is verifying those assumptions. And it's sort of like raising kids; you get one shot at it." On the other hand, this job requires the most immediate kind of focus, the ability to take a shapeless hunk of sea rock and slowly reveal what's inside—a bayonet hilt, perhaps, or a mercury gauge or an engine register. "One of the great frustrations of this is that things only happen one at a time. If I'm not working on the engine, I'm working on this," he says, pointing to rows of small tubs filled with artifacts awaiting his study.

It will take a long time, maybe decades, to conserve all the artifacts recovered from the *Monitor*. The twenty-foot-wide turret, which was perhaps the ship's most enduring innovation, was recovered during the summer of 2002 and brought to the museum. The engine alone could keep one gearhead busy for years and years. But standing by the 91,000-gallon treatment tank where it sits, Curtiss Peterson seems to be in his own rusty corner of heaven. "This is eating the elephant, right?" he says. "One bite at a time."

FREEDOM'S FORTRESS

On the wide, grassy ribbon that wraps around the top of Fort Monroe, the daffodils sway and nod solemnly over the graves. They're just not the graves you'd expect. "Juggernaut, Oct. 14, 1969-Sept. 21, 1982. A stout fellow. The Campbells." "Winkie Mace Whittington, 1941-1954, Beloved companion and world traveler." "Gallant Dog Jeb, 1940-1954." Lady and Blue, Puffin and Snickerdoodle. Stone after stone embedded in the grass of this historic fort overlooking Hampton Roads, wedged between the half-moons of iron where the heels of massive guns once swung, the simple names and sentiments are a unique testament to the humanity that

exists at the center of conflict. Though always military in nature and purpose, a fort is also a place where people live their lives, and throughout its storied history, Fort Monroe has been a remarkably beautiful haven, an oddly peaceful place.

Even in the midst of the Civil War—when Fort Monroe proved its strategic worth as a Union stronghold in the heart of the Confederacy—willows, oaks, cedars and magnolias graced its interior, shading the stately homes of the officers, dulling the thud of guns. "For hours every night the skies are a moving panorama of pictures, continually changing, of sunshine and shadow, light and shade, and deeply dyed with every color of the rainbow," Verna Winchester wrote her cousin in November 1861. "When the music of the *Minnesota's* band comes in at your casement, mellowed by the distance and you watch across the waters the fading of those lovely tints as twilight deepens then—

imagine the rest Ella. I am not sentimental today, and language fails me."
When you stand atop Fort Monroe today, Winchester's warm description
(recounted in John V. Quarstein and Dennis Mroczkowski's *Fort Monroe, The
Key to the South*) still rings true. And to walk through this fort's massive gates
on a hushed summer evening, the air heavy with seabreeze and cicadas, is to
walk through a door into another time.

The fort standing today is a relatively new kid on the block. So strategically
located is Old Point Comfort that even the earliest settlers realized its defen-
sive value. Algernourne Fort was built here in 1609, followed by two more in
the mid-1600s, and then Fort George, begun in 1728. Despite its sixteen-foot-
thick walls, Fort George fell to a hurricane in 1749. In 1802, the government
built the lighthouse at Old Point Comfort (still standing at Fort Monroe
today), but nothing was there to stop the British from waltzing into the
basically defenseless Chesapeake Bay during the War of 1812 and sacking
Hampton. It wasn't long after that harsh lesson—1819 in fact—that the walls
started going up at Fort Monroe. Designed by Frenchman Simon Bernard, the
fort named for President James Monroe was built to prevent such an attack
from happening again. Its granite walls were up to fifty feet thick and as high
as thirty-five feet above the moat—which ranged from 75 to 150 feet across—
surrounding it. In his drawing of the fort in 1862, Private Robert Knox Sneden
noted of the moat that the tide "ebbs and flows in [the] ditch 8 to 15 feet
daily." A rough hexagon, its corners protruded in diamond shapes so that
every inch of its outer walls could be peppered with crossfire. It comprised
sixty-three acres, accommodated 412 guns, and could house more than 2,600
men. It remains the largest moat-encircled stone fort in the nation.

Though built to defend the fledgling nation from outside attack, Fort
Monroe is most famous for its role in the Civil War. It enabled the Union to
establish the blockading fleet at the port of Hampton Roads at the entrance to
Chesapeake Bay, was the launching point for several major naval operations
in the south, and was the base for General George McClellan's march north
toward Richmond. Soldiers, families and officers watched from its walls as the
ironclads *Monitor* and *Virginia* dueled. President Abraham Lincoln, annoyed
with the Union navy's inability to get up the James River and at McClellan's
apparent foot-dragging on the peninsula, came to the fort in May 1862. He
held a council of war in the fort's Old Quarters No. 1 (its two tiers of ginger-
bread-decorated porches ensuring that today it remains one of the loveliest
buildings in the fort), and even went out in a small boat and conducted his
own assessment of the coastline across Hampton Roads to decide how the
Union could kick the Confederates out of Norfolk.

The fort earned its name "Freedom's Fortress" for its role in defining
slavery as a legitimate question in the war. When Union soldiers marched
into neighboring Hampton to disrupt the town's vote for secession, a

handful of slaves escaped into Union hands. When their owner demanded their return, Major General Benjamin Franklin Butler, who had taken command of the fort in May 1861, refused. He knew the slaves were being used to help the Confederates, so he called them "contraband of war." Dozens more escaped, and Butler put the runaways to work helping build up the Union defenses, providing them with housing, food, clothing and wages in return. Though Butler's decision was initially considered radical, by August Congress formally approved the approach of keeping slaves that had worked against the Union, making slavery a major wartime issue. Fort Monroe's Civil War fame was assured when captured Confederate President Jefferson Davis was imprisoned in Casemate No. 2 in May 1865. Davis was charged with treason and implicated in Lincoln's assassination, but ultimately stood trial for neither.

Today, while it remains a working military installation, everything surrounding Fort Monroe has changed, and perhaps that's what makes walking through its low-ceilinged, stone casemates (artillery housings) and along its walls such a time-shifting experience. A chunk of the fort is dedicated to the Casemate Museum, which describes the fort's history and is filled with photos depicting soldier and family life. Among the artifacts are Davis's Meerschaum pipe, its bowl clutched in the claw of an eagle, and a cribbage board carried by one Sergeant C.C. Pratt of the 20th Maine Regiment of Infantry. Battle flags, encased in glass, are scarred and torn, their myriad stories of courage and sadness told in the faded letters upon their stripes—Antietam, Fredericksburg, Gettysburg, Bull Run. The names seem to burn over the chasm of years.

Here in the casemates are Davis's cell, which in a fading afternoon doesn't seem so bad with its whitewashed walls and the sunlight reflecting off the moat, glancing through the single, barred window at the embrasure and flickering like flame along the vaulted ceiling. Several of the fort's casemates were remodeled into living quarters for families, and so what was built as a home for cannon was transformed—with wood paneling and floors, a fireplace, curtains, rocking chairs and a claw-footed table draped in a lace tablecloth—into a most unlikely, yet cozy, dwelling for officers and their brides.

Nowhere, though, is Fort Monroe more frozen in time than upon its ramparts and terrepleine—the narrow swath of green where dozens of Rodman guns once pounded, where Jeff Davis walked to improve his fragile health while a prisoner, where hundreds of soldiers and civilians watched the fearful burning of Union warships as the C.S.S. Virginia laid waste to the fleet, where Lincoln gazed across the broad water, perhaps lifting his long, burdened face to the soothing breeze off the Bay, where over the generations soldiers' families have laid to rest their beloved pets. Here, you place one

Photograph courtesy of Fort Monroe

Old Point Comfort Lighthouse

In 1774, at the entrance to Hampton Roads harbor where Fort Monroe would later rise, stone masons began building the fifty-four foot sandstone tower that would be known as Old Point Comfort lighthouse. Lit in 1802, the light is still operational after being automated in 1972. White with a green lantern room and distinctive red roof, this charming and historic lighthouse is the second oldest beacon on the Chesapeake Bay. It was restored after being badly damaged during the Civil War and today is listed on the National Register of Historic Places. The adjacent wood-frame keeper's cottage was built in 1900 and reflects the Victorian architecture of the time. Both the lighthouse and the cottage are open to the public.

foot in front of the other and walk a path where General John Ellis Wool, who took command of the fort in August 1861, gazed out at scores of warships, sails furled, resting at anchor. And more than a century later, here you watch as two soldiers stand at attention before the American flag streaming in the southerly breeze as "Retreat" and "To the Colors" is played at day's end, while a fishing trawler heads seaward beyond the fort's walls, its downriggers outstretched like long arms waving to the water. ▪

SAVING THE NATIVES

In the mossy damp grotto that is the woodland floodplain of Adkins Arboretum, spring peepers trill a pure song of hope and desire. Songbirds flit through the low branches, and along the gentle banks of the Piney Branch the rich green forest floor is alight in spring beauties, tiny stars of white flowers, shot through with pink. No manmade sanctuary could be this peaceful, so full of spring's quiet promise of rebirth. And yet, Ellie Altman is frowning. She bends down along the path and gently cups the bloom of a spring beauty like a mother lifting her daughter's face, then points to what appears to be an inconsequential green-leafed vine sprouting right next to the flower. "See, this is the challenge here," she says. "You don't want to come in here and spray this with Roundup because you'll kill the flower. But if you dig the honeysuckle up and prune the roots, the roots will just multiply." She shakes her head disapprovingly, looking for a moment like a second-grade teacher deeply disappointed with some half-pint repeat offender. Perhaps you always thought kindly of honeysuckle—Japanese honeysuckle, to be exact—even licked the sweet nectar from its yellow and white blooms and reveled in its perfume on the breeze. But after a visit to Adkins Arboretum, you will never see it the same way again. For it is an interloper, an aggressive outsider who shoves aside the more timid and demure flowers and plants that have called this woodland home for centuries. Truth be told, the ubiquitous vine that smells like spun gold and crawls all over the Chesapeake countryside is nothing better than a streetwise bully.

Little revelations like this are what make Adkins Arboretum, located in Ridgely, Maryland, on the middle Eastern Shore, so much fun—and so important. No other arboretum does what it does: focuses exclusively on the conservation of nontidal plants native to the central Delmarva Peninsula. With its miles of tranquil footpaths wending among fields, meadows, upland woods and floodplain woodlands, Adkins is a living museum of flora that has evolved here over generations. Ellie Altman, its executive director, and her staff are creating a place where adults and children can learn about plants, flowers, trees, shrubs and grasses vital to the Chesapeake Bay's ecosystem, and why the preservation and propagation of native species is gaining momentum as a measure of the Bay's genetic heritage and health. Education can be as simple as a self-guided walking tour through the woods or as involved as a three-day seminar for home gardeners on how and why to use native plants in gardens and landscaping. "It's unusual for an arboretum to focus on native plants, and our displays are of plants in their natural setting, so we're teaching the ecology of the area," Altman says. "It's not what most people expect from a botanic garden."

This mission was something Adkins grew into. Maryland's Department of Natural Resources in 1972 proposed a state arboretum within the 4,000-acre

Tuckahoe State Park. The original plan was rather typical (and ultimately unrealistic)—a traditional showcase of all Maryland trees—and called for creating an 800-acre lake by building a dam at Hillsboro. Thankfully for what is now Adkins' extensive and beautiful woodland floodplain, the plan was abandoned, and the arboretum largely lay fallow. In 1979, local resident and tree-lover Leon Andrus created an endowment for the arboretum, and the Friends of Adkins Arboretum, a private foundation, formed to manage it. In 1998, the state agreed to a fifty-year lease with the foundation, handing it the reins of the arboretum's development and stewardship. "Even though this facility is twenty years old, it's very young because it sat here for a decade," says Altman, who was named executive director shortly after the foundation took over the place.

Adkins now comprises 400 acres, bordered on the west by Tuckahoe Creek and perforated with its tributaries, Piney Branch and Blockston Branch creeks. More than 600 species of flora thrive here. "I think what makes this place special," says

Altman, "is we have this story to tell about land conservation upstream. Most organizations are talking about conservation at the water's edge." Walking Adkins's woods leads visitors among swamp magnolias, beech trees, tulip poplars and hollies looming over paw paw, skunk cabbage, mayapples and ragwort. In the uplands, land that was plowed some thirty years ago is now home to a young forest of Virginia pine, loblolly, red cedar and river birch (and a vast carpet of the voracious Japanese honeysuckle). From there, the path leads back to a meadow golden with broom sedge, and the wetlands that surround the visitor center. Throughout, subtle signs invite visitors to read the self-guided tour map and learn more about what they are seeing.

The walk through the woods is gorgeous, and its gentle purpose doesn't go unnoticed. It's not unusual, Altman says, for someone to ask why something

like Japanese honeysuckle, which has grown on their property for fifty years, doesn't qualify as "native." She laughs. "It's not like antiques," she says. "Just because something has been here a hundred years doesn't make it native. It's an issue of having evolved here naturally." Adkins's staff defines natives as "plants that have evolved here without human introduction for 10,000 years—since the last Ice Age." They can determine these species through the work of early botanists, as well as with modern research techniques like carbon dating and soil boring.

Of the 600 species at Adkins, about 20 percent are non-natives, some more problemmatical than others. Along with Japanese honeysuckle, which simply overruns and strangles less aggressive plants, other gangsters of the Delmarva plant world are Queen Anne's lace and all those daylilies you see blooming on rural roadsides. Loosestrife, which gardeners innocently plant for its lovely purple flowers, in the wild will overtake wetlands. Ivy that climbs elegantly up trees will eventually kill them with its blanket of shade. The multiflora rose that looks so delicate rampages throughout the upland landscape. Slowly but surely eradicating these intruders is one of Adkins's missions. Each plant requires a different approach. For example, Altman says, the spotted knapweed, which produces its pretty violet flower every other year, gets cut toward the end of every summer to prevent it from going to seed. Multiflora rose is cut to the nub and then gets its stump painted with Roundup, (the herbicide of choice, since it does not spread into the soil, instead working systemically within a plant to kill it). "Ivy we've just dug out," says Altman. And as for the rapacious honeysuckle, she can't resist ripping a few strands out as she walks along the woods path.

It isn't always easy making people appreciate the inherent value of a diminutive woodland flower or even a plant someone grew up thinking was no better than a weed. So the arboretum has started its own sort of cultivation to spread the word. Its experts conduct off-campus seminars for home gardeners on the idea of native gardens—what's called conservation landscaping or sustainable horticulture. Programs for young kids include identifying different animal tracks and exploring the origins of snowflakes. At Halloween, thousands of people take part in the haunted hayride through the woods, and at Christmas the paths are lit with candles for carolers to serenade the trees and each other. An annual arboretum art competition encourages regional artists to focus on plant and landscape themes. The University of Maryland's Master Gardener program uses the arboretum to train students, and many of them go on to become museum volunteers—a critical job, since the arboretum only has five full-time staff. And every spring and fall, the arboretum holds sales of native plants—many of which are grown from local seed and propagated in the arboretum's nursery.

And still, there is much to learn. Ellie Altman stops along the woodland trail and bends down to a low carpet of feathery green foliage. "Creeping cedar," she says. "You won't see it in nurseries, because we don't know how to propagate it." She brushes her hands over the little mystery, while the peepers sing their spring song. ■

Adkins Arboretum

Adkins Arboretum is a Chesapeake Bay Gateways Network site near the headwaters of the Tuckahoe River. Its location exemplifies the natural landscape along a headwater stream on the Chesapeake Bay's Eastern Shore. Other nearby Gateways sites include Tuckahoe State Park.

TUCKAHOE

You cannot walk the shores of the Chesapeake Bay or travel its tributaries without treading on history. It's all here—shark teeth from the Miocene Epoch 10 million to 20 million years ago, stone tools from paleo-Indian tribes, lost towns whose names are whispers in time, colonial plantation homes still shaded in magnolias, Revolutionary forts, sad, simple graves of Civil War dead. In many places on the Bay, the modern world of highways and strip malls tramples on and obscures this past. But in the quiet solitude of Tuckahoe River on Maryland's upper Eastern Shore, you can, quite simply, time travel.

Photograph courtesy of Michael Wootton

This is what Carl Scheffel is doing on a fine autumn day, though to the uninitiated it seems he is just paddling his small dory down the broad back of the river. To fold yourself into a small boat, though, and silently travel the sinuous path this waterway has carved for thousands of years is to open yourself to the possibilities of a tangible, reachable past. Scheffel, executive director of the Old Harford Town Maritime Center in nearby Denton, Maryland, comes here often to get an unadulterated feel for what once was. Some twenty-five miles long from its mouth on the upper Choptank River to its navigable end north of Hillsboro, the Tuckahoe squirms like a snake into the Delmarva hinterland. Native Americans hunted and fished its banks and woodlands as long as 10,000 years ago. Frederick Douglass, who helped awaken a nation to the inhumanity and degradation of slavery, spent his early years exploring its shores. One hundred-fifty years ago, the Tuckahoe was a veritable riverine highway, a thriving trade route for steamboats that negotiated its tight turns and powerful currents to land at wharves named Wayman and New Bridge, Cowards and Coveys, moving goods and people between the Eastern Shore and Baltimore.

Today the river is silent, save for the keen of an osprey or the prehistoric squawk of a blue heron. Though it's still remarkably deep for a skinny Eastern Shore waterway—in some places as much as thirty feet—the only boats that venture up here are small runabouts carrying fishermen, or kayaks and canoes. Twisting and turning, the river carries a powerful current that drops the water as much as four feet on a falling tide. The riverscape is a layered mosaic. Floating meadows of yellow pond lilies border broad fields of reeds and grasses, which give way to a low shoreline topped with mile after mile of oaks and sycamores, maples and sweet gums. It would seem, in all this unmolested solitude, that the river's busy past could not possibly be real. But traces of it are still here to touch, if you know what to reach for.

Scheffel maneuvers his dory over to the western shoreline, passing muscular, gnarled tree roots and fallen limbs. Eventually he points his bow toward a slit of water trickling into the river, and as he paddles into the woods on the nearly hidden stream covered with autumn leaves, he seems to be floating on gold. On either side, steep banks climb forty feet to a plateau ringed in oaks and maples. Sunlight slants through the treetops, and there's no sound but the creak of late autumn crickets, birdsong, and the occasional rustle of leaves as a fox or squirrel skitters from Scheffel's presence. This is Kentucky Ravine, and on its edge, in a rough wooden cabin, is where Frederick Douglass was born in 1818. Here he spent the first six years of his life under the loving care of his grandmother before he was torn from all he knew and marched twelve miles to the home of his master, Aaron Anthony, where he began to understand the ugly reality that he was a slave. "The old cabin, with its rail floor and rail bedsteads upstairs, and its clay floor downstairs, and its dirt chimney and windowless sides, and that most curious piece of workmanship dug out in front of the fireplace, beneath which grandmammy placed the sweet potatoes to keep them from the frost, was *my home*, the only home I ever had, and I loved it, and all connected with it," Douglass wrote in *My Bondage and My Freedom*. "The old fences around it, and the stumps in the edge of the woods near it, and the squirrels that ran, skipped and played upon them, were objects of interest and affection. … Where could such another home be met with?"

If you come here looking for a chunk of chimney or corner of foundation, you will be disappointed. Though Douglass returned to this spot in 1878 and proclaimed it the site of his birth, grabbing a handful of earth to take with him, there's no visible trace of the cabin he loved. But time has not changed the stark, quiet peace of the place. Sitting here next to the clear running stream, sunlight dappling the leaves, it is entirely possible to leave the contemporary world behind and travel a straight channel back. The rich, woody muck of the riverside smells the same as it did when Douglass' grandmother, Betsey Bailey, worked her seine nets along the Tuckahoe's banks. The red oaks and maples still drop their leaves to flutter in the soft breeze, and the minnows still flicker in the creek shallows, as they did when Native Americans camped and hunted on these shores.

The tide is falling, and Scheffel's dory bumps the bottom of the skinny creek as he wiggles his way out of Kentucky Ravine and back into the

Tuckahoe. Upstream about half a mile, he rounds a 90° curve in the river and comes upon the skeletal remains of a wharf. At high tide, all that's visible are innocuous hummocks of grass sprouting from the piling stubs like weedy wigs. On a low tide, the full extent of the structure stretches just off the shoreline for some 300 feet downstream. This is what's left of Wayman Wharf, one of the busiest steamboat stops on the Tuckahoe.

From at least 1881, this was as far upstream as steamships could navigate. They would tie up here and wait for smaller craft called lighters to take their loads another two-and-a-half miles north to Hillsboro. Caleb C. Wheeler, who established the Wheeler Transportation Line on the Tuckahoe in the late 1870s, rented this wharf from the Wayman family for $40 a year, and his boats—among them the 124-foot *Ruggles* and the 130-foot *Minnie Wheeler*— were regular callers from Baltimore. In 1881, passengers would pay fifty cents for a cabin on the *Minnie Wheeler* from Baltimore to Hillsboro—another fifty cents for a stateroom and an extra half-dollar for meals. They would leave Baltimore at seven in the evening and travel south down the Bay and up the Choptank River through the night, awakening to the sun rising over the treetops as the boat turned up the Tuckahoe. By nine in the morning, the ship would be snugged tight to the pier against the relentless pull of the river, the road down to the wharf busy with wagons and horses, farmers delivering loads of grain and peaches, and children darting underfoot.

In the late afternoon of an autumn day in the early twenty-first century, all this commerce and bustle simply does not seem possible in this forgotten, silent place. But as you touch the ragged pilings, the past rough and wet beneath your fingers, you are suddenly not so far from that busy, long-distant scene. Archaeologists and historians can describe how people built their homes, gathered their food and lived their lives. Old photos of steamboats chuffing their way up rivers, and wharves loaded with waiting livestock and passengers document a vanished past. But only in a place like this can you remove the distance of time and open your senses and imagination to their world as it was. Such is the wonder of time travel on the Tuckahoe. ■

Choptank & Tuckahoe Rivers Water Trail

The gentle Tuckahoe River flows into its sister waterway, the Choptank—the Eastern Shore's longest river. Collectively they meander for more than eighty miles, much of the distance encompassed today by the Choptank and Tuckahoe Rivers Water Trail. This classic Chesapeake Bay landscape, with its typical vegetation of grasses, shrubs, and low-growing trees, once was the backdrop for a bustling maritime commerce. Vestiges of this vibrant past are still discernable today, making a paddle down the rivers an exploration both of nature and a slice of Bay history.

HIDDEN HISTORY

The Tuckahoe River squirms like a scared snake through the flatlands of Maryland's Eastern Shore, its ferocious current scouring the deep bottom curves and piling the silt along its lily-covered flats. Bruce Thompson and his team of volunteer divers have waited since morning for the tide to settle down, and now it's time to slip into the river and search its mysteries. "All I want you to do is go down the anchor line, feel for wood and come back up and tell me what you've got," Thompson tells the three sitting on the small boat's gunwale, spitting into their masks. "The big thing I need is your general impressions of the site. Stay close to the anchor, feel for timbers, fasteners, see if there are any artifacts or articulated timbers." The three nod and one by one fall over backwards into the coffee-colored water. They bob on the surface, faces turned toward Thompson awaiting the go-ahead. "Stay together," he tells them. "Hold hands."

All dives are tricky, but this one is a doozy. The river is about twenty-eight feet deep here, and black as a coal bunker. Once the three get to the bottom, their hands will be their only eyes. And what they're trying to feel and see is a shipwreck. All they know about it is what Thompson knows, and at this point, that isn't much. As assistant underwater archaeologist for the state of Maryland, Thompson has been over this patch of water before with side-scan sonar, and what he saw told him he needed to dive on it to learn more. He hopes it's a steamboat from the late 1800s, when this river was a commercial workhorse; he suspects it's more likely a barge from the same era. There's a good chance he'll never know for sure. The rivers and the Bay guard their phantoms well, hiding them deep in the silt and murk of time and tide. At best, he may only have the ghostly outline on the side-scan, maybe a timber or fastener or two. Doesn't he ever wish he could see it, intact? Thompson smiles through his bushy beard, a Marlboro Light poking from one corner of his mouth. His laugh is like the growl of a friendly bear. He points between his eyes. "I see it in here," he says. "I've touched so many frames, I've romanced frames in my dreams. It's easy for me to hold a ship in my mind."

Since 1989, Thompson has traveled the Chesapeake's darkest waters in search of the past. He, Susan Langley and Steve Bilicki are the backbone of the Maryland Maritime Archaeology Program (MMAP), a part of the Maryland Historical Trust. In 1988, Maryland's legislature passed the Submerged Archaeological Historic Property Act, which established MMAP as part of the state Office of Archaeology. The program's goals are ambitious: to identify, map, study and manage all of the state's historically significant underwater sites; to protect sites by reviewing all Army Corps of Engineers permits for waterfront development; and to develop research and education programs with state universities. "One reason we're doing this is not just to identify fancy wrecks," Thompson says. "If a developer comes in and wants to change a whole site, we say, 'No boys, you've got to do a whole survey … If it's going

to be on a shipwreck or a shell midden we can ask them to move it. If they can't do that, we require them to do certain surveys."

Lastly, the program is mandated to entice the public, especially sport divers, to volunteer, and that's a critical mission, Thompson says. Every day, erosion, sedimentation and development wash away, dig up or bury pieces of Maryland's submerged history. With more than 4,430 miles of shoreline and hundreds of historic sites, three archaeologists can't possibly do it all. Thompson works with about ninety volunteers, though his rock solid group—those who always manage to put in the hours and weeks doing everything from wreck diving to researching historical records to cataloging artifacts—numbers about fifteen.

The volunteers are an eclectic assortment—scientists, lawyers, engineers, students, machinists, business owners. "One of the great things about Maryland is that we have such a technological base here, ninety percent of our volunteers are really well educated," Thompson says. Betty Colhoun, a systems engineer on the Hubble space telescope, started diving with Bruce after he found remains of the colonial-era Stephen Steward Shipyard on the West River, right around the corner from Colhoun's farm. "My husband's family were partners in the ships built at the yard," she says. "They were traders, so probably one of their ships is lying someplace under here." She was so intrigued by the history and the archaeology, she signed up for a dive class and within a year was one of Thompson's top volunteers. Nothing seems to faze her—not diving in black water, not spending hours up to her shoulders in muck, not driving MMAP's careening white truck loaded to the gills with gear. "I'm having a ball," she says.

Working with Bruce Thompson is a combination of the deadly serious—especially when diving—and rollicking camaraderie, with plenty of esoteric discussion, debate, history and storytelling thrown in. "I just like hanging around this guy," says John Lewis, a retired businessman from Annapolis who is renowned among the volunteer cadre for his "perfects"— Manhattans he serves when the day is done and everyone is hanging around, talking about the day's work and whatever else comes up. Mitch Grieb, who owns a machining company in Chestertown, routinely offers his house for volunteers to stay at while working on extended dives in the area. He began working with Bruce after his late father found several extraordinary seventeenth and eighteenth-century sites on his farm.

As of 2002, MMAP had surveyed portions of all of the state's twenty-four rivers, locating about 500 historic and prehistoric sites. Among them are the Steward Shipyard; Maryland's first underwater dive preserve, the wreck of German U-boat *Black Panther* lying in eighty-six feet of water just off Piney Point in the Potomac River; the lost flotilla of Commodore Joshua Barney, who defended the Potomac River against the British in the War of 1812; and a Native American site on the Port Tobacco River that yielded pottery shards dating to 285 to 100 B.C. Archaeologist Steve Bilicki has used side-scan sonar and magnetometers to locate the remains of Fort Horn, one of Annapolis's earliest defenses, now underwater a few hundred yards off the tip of Horn Point.

While Maryland waters are replete with historic sites and wrecks, Thompson's darling is the Eastern Shore. Archaeologists haven't paid as much attention to it as the western shore, but Thompson's imagination—which is always working overtime—is captivated with the written and oral history of the places here, the lost towns like Claiborne and New Yarmouth. "They had a shipyard, too," he grins, his eyebrows jumping. Over the last twelve years, Bruce Thompson and his cadre have covered 5,114 acres of the shore's waters, walked 817 acres of its shorelines and spent hours in the stacks researching the histories. Among his favorite finds have been a log canoe that dates from the late 1700s, which had lain buried in sand and silt for generations until erosion uncovered part of its bow. Because it was in danger of being damaged by winter storms, Thompson excavated the canoe, which has now been conserved and is being reassembled at the Maryland

Archaelogical Conservation Lab. In most cases, Thompson leaves artifacts where he finds them, and requires that his volunteers do the same. "Take nothing, leave nothing," he says. "Unless they're going to tell you something, leave them." An exception, he says, is when a significant artifact is in danger of being destroyed or has been so exposed it could be taken by someone.

Back on the Tuckahoe, Thompson's three volunteers, Betty Colhoun among them, have surfaced and are reporting in. "I thought I felt the bow, sticking up about four feet," says Tim Sayre. "It was loose, I was rocking it." There's no visibility, he says, but the bottom seems firm. Thompson quizzes them some more; part of his goal today is to get these divers acclimated to this site, so that when they return tomorrow they will have a better mental image of what they're hunting for. "The current's starting to shift, so when you feel it really starting to cook, come on up," Thompson tells them. "Go up to the bow and see if you can feel curvature on the other side. Then feel inside, see if you can feel frames." The three signal okay and disappear again. Thompson scribbles some notes, sucks on another cigarette, and wonders about the hidden history below, whether the river will give up her secrets to the man who loves to dream of them. ■

A LOVE OF OLD THINGS

It is a sparkling day at the Chesapeake Bay Maritime Museum in Saint Michaels, Maryland, and no one is sitting still. Teenagers charge up the steps of the 123-year-old Hooper Strait Lighthouse and imagine the life of a lighthouse keeper. Toddlers climb into the pilothouse of the buyboat *Thor*, spin the steering wheel and scramble into the cozy bunk behind the helm. In the museum's boat shop, artisans are restoring a wooden skiff. In the harbor, the gorgeous log canoe *Edna E. Lockwood*, built in 1889 on Tilghman Island, seems to fly where she floats. And on the skipjack *Rosie Parks*, men run their hands over wooden spars and wonder what it must feel like to sail her on a frigid winter's morning, dredging for oysters. In the center of it all sits the elegant Tolchester Beach Bandstand, built in 1880 in the age of steamboats and gentility, and if Vida Van Lennep were visiting the museum on this day, one might expect her to be taking in the shade here, her long legs crossed primly. On the other hand, that would presume that ninety-two-year-old Vida Van Lennep might want to sit still. And

that is not something this woman—whose inspiration and motivation helped create this remarkable museum dedicated to Bay culture—has ever done.

It's one of life's little ironies that the woman behind this museum isn't even from here. She and her husband, Gus Van Lennep Jr., were from Philadelphia. They had met in Cape May on the Jersey shore, fell in love on a sailboat, and it was a sailboat that brought them to Saint Michaels and the Chesapeake. Specifically, a thirty-seven-foot gaff-rigged beauty called *Elf*, built in 1888 by the renown Boston boatbuilder George Lawley. "When we were married in 1931 we were given a nest egg of a thousand dollars, and we saw an ad in *Yachting*, and, well, there she is," she says, pointing to a painting hanging near her door of a sharp little boat biting the breeze. "There went our nest egg, plus two hundred dollars." They also saw an ad in *Yachting* for a reputable boatbuilder in Oxford, and so after doing what they could with her themselves, they sailed *Elf* to the Bay for some extensive work. "We just fell in love with it. Saint Michaels was a dear little town. The side streets were all oyster shell. The houses were wood and most of them didn't have much paint. It was a watermen's town and I guess they didn't have time to paint."

For two people who found grace in age and beauty beneath the rough exteriors, the small Eastern Shore town quickly became home. In 1937 they moved for good and bought Rolles Range, a home built in 1751. "'We like old houses—we're a little nutty that way," she says, speaking of Gus as though he is in the room with her, though he died several years ago. "We just like old things." A few years later they bought Crooked Intention, a farmhouse dating from 1710. "All the original paneling was there, so we were intrigued. It needed everything, but we were just young enough and nutty enough to do it." Vida had attended the Philadelphia School of Industrial Art and the Pennsylvania Academy of Fine Arts, and Gus was a lawyer by training. But when they came to Saint Michaels they ended up restoring old houses, farming, churning butter and cooking on a coal range. One year, Vida says, Gus had an oyster boat built, named it *Retriever* and went oystering. Just to see what it was like.

It was probably inevitable that their love of "old things," as Vida calls them, as well as their passion for hard-working boats, got them thinking about a museum devoted to the Bay's maritime heritage. "It got started because there wasn't one," she says simply. Though The Mariners' Museum in Newport News, Virginia, had an exhibit about the Bay, its focus was far broader. Nowhere was there a museum devoted only to Bay craft and culture. So they started doing their homework. They visited The Mariners' Museum and soaked up the valuable experience of its then-curator Robert Burgess. They went to Mystic Seaport and consulted with the Maryland Historic Trust, which literally opened up its basement to them to borrow musty old maritime artifacts. Then they made the museum happen.

"She was the catalyst, she and Gus," says John Valliant, now the museum's director. "Without their continued energy and enthusiasm and pushing things, it probably would have just plodded along. It really took off as a result of their involvement." In the museum archives is a yellowed newspaper clipping showing an eager young Valliant, in sixth grade, handing over a check to the handsome Gus Van Lennep, vice president of the Historic Society of Talbot County. The class won the money for its Johnny Appleseed float in the Halloween Parade, and they donated it to the fledgling museum.

In 1963, the Historic Society of Talbot County agreed to develop the museum, formed an organizing committee and raised $50,000 to purchase three old buildings on the Saint Michaels waterfront that would become its nucleus. "A sudden awakening has taken place to the fact that the bugeye, the skipjack, the log sailing canoe, the pungy, the sharpie, the schooner, the sloop, the crab skiff, the batteau, the brogan would in the not-too-distant future become things of the past," the organizing committee wrote in its prospectus. "So why not do something to preserve them in a museum, on land and on water? Thus tribute would be paid to these vessels and their functioning, and to the men who built and sailed them."

Vida, in a *Washington Star* story published March 28, 1965, put it more succinctly: "We want to save what we can, at a time when things are dropping out of sight overnight." As head of the curator's committee, she put out the call that would soon overrun her house with models and books, binnacles and tools. Today, she laughs about trying to stumble around her home without breaking her neck as she frantically stacked up piece after precious piece, waiting for renovations on the museum's buildings to finish so she could install the beginning of its collection. "Our house was so full of stuff we couldn't entertain or anything," she says, "but it was a lot of fun."

Among those early donations were a fifty-five-foot Alden yawl (later sold), an 1895 log canoe, an early 1900s binnacle from the Annapolis sidewheeler *Gov. Emerson E. Harrington*, lanterns, models and watermen's tools. And best of all, the oyster schooner *J.T. Leonard*, built in 1882 on Taylors Island, on loan during the off season. When the museum opened on a shining spring day, May 22, 1965, with some 1,500 people looking on, including state and federal dignitaries, the long bowsprit of the *Leonard* was in the foreground of nearly every photo, tied up along the bulkhead right in front of the new museum. The photos ran in newspapers as venerable as the *New York Times* and as far afield as the *Columbus Dispatch* in Ohio. Saint Michaels was suddenly on the map.

Of course, that was only a beginning. The museum had no paid staff, and so Vida signed on as a full-time volunteer curator. Under her inspired leadership and wide open mind, the museum bloomed like a shadbush in spring. In the archives today are dozens of photos of her, usually surrounded by a cadre of men, accepting a log canoe model or a check or a cache of historic photographs. Invariably she stands straight-backed, her feet together just so, wearing a stylish skirt or dress and jacket and a smile on her face. She hadn't been curator a year before she snapped up what remains the museum's showstopper, the Hooper Strait Lighthouse. The Coast Guard was decommissioning most of the Bay's old lighthouses, and Hooper Strait had stood watch over Tangier Sound since the late 1870s. Its charming cottage architecture was pure Chesapeake Bay. It weighed forty tons and would be sawn in half, disconnected from its pilings and barged up the Bay to its new home on Navy Point. It was a crazy idea. Vida loved it. "It was a big order, that's true," she says. "But it seemed then like anything could happen." When the barge hove into view on a late autumn day in 1966, most of the town showed up to watch, and the schools let the kids out to witness the amazing sight. "It was just sort of breathtaking," she says. "It looked like an old six-sided sugar bowl. They took the top off and set it on the side with the finial on top. That's exactly what it looked like."

Aside from the lighthouse's historical value, it was a brilliant public relations move—the old lighthouse, and the town and museum were written up in magazines and countless newspapers. By 1969, the museum achieved independence from the Historic Society of Talbot County, and had attracted

Hooper Strait lighthouse

**Chesapeake Bay
Maritime Museum**

The Hooper Strait lighthouse
is a fine example of a screwpile
light, the "signature" lighthouse
style of the Chesapeake Bay.
Developed in England in
the eighteenth century, the
screwpile form consisted of
a hexagonal or cylindrical
cottage set on a wooden
or iron framework of spiderlike
legs that could be screwed
into the bottom of a shoal.
Screwpiles seemed ideal for
locations where erosion or
other conditions made an
onshore light unfeasible, and
many of them were erected
in shallow parts of the Bay.
In winter the structures were
vulnerable to floating ice,
however, and over time several
were ripped from their foundations or otherwise damaged
beyond repair. In its new home
at the Chesapeake Bay Maritime
Museum, and beautifully
restored, the Hooper Strait light
harkens back to a pre-electronic
era when lighthouses were
essential to guiding mariners
safely through the Bay.

more than 100,000 visitors. In November of that year, it hired its first full-time curator and director, and Vida quietly moved into the background. Today, the museum owns eighteen acres and has nine exhibit buildings and 7,000 members. More than 91,000 people visit annually. Its collection includes 8,000 artifacts, 85 boats, 2,700 photos, 220 oral histories, 73 manuscript collections and an 8,900-volume library. Its auditorium is named after Vida and Gus Van Lennep.

Vida lives quietly in nearby Easton, in a modern home full of lovely old things, like the eighteenth-century mantelpiece over the fireplace and the Schoenhutt dolls she painstakingly restores. She still sits up straight like a proper lady, dresses with style, has a ready sense of humor and may be inclined to call you "dearie"—and you won't mind a bit. Having seen all that has changed on the Chesapeake in nearly seventy years, she is grateful she and Gus never gave up on their dream of a place dedicated to the Bay's maritime culture and past. And so, most definitely, are a lot of other people. ■

Window on the Chesapeake

LIFE IN EVERY DETAIL

Barnacles. They don't look like much, cemented to pilings and oyster shells and rocks, soundless dwellers on the tidal fringes of the Chesapeake Bay. You might not even notice them until you shred your foot on one. Then you'd limp away, grumbling a blue opinion of the little bugger's crusty shell, never knowing what you missed.

A.J. Lippson, on the other hand, misses very little. Her eye is attuned to the living wonders of the Bay, and her hand is well versed in their rendering. As a gifted and award-winning biological illustrator, her drawings of Bay creatures, from the fiercely majestic osprey to the obscure freckled paddle worm, reveal a world most never see closely, if at all. The humble barnacle, for instance. To the unobservant or impatient, it looks like nothing so much as a ragged chunk of tooth, inanimate and dull. Yet A.J.'s series of black and white drawings of a barnacle underwater unveils a strangely graceful creature. Cautiously opening the roof of its immobile home, it unfurls a fan of feathery appendages that caress the water, sweeping food inside. It looks like nothing so much as a sensuous fan dance, a slow-motion swirl and swish of a flamenco dancer's skirt. The "plain old barnacle," as she terms it, is one of A.J.'s favorites. So are mantis shrimp. And worms: Parchment worms and bamboo worms, the milky ribbon worm and the clam worm. All part of the mysterious and intricate network of animals that make up the Bay's delicate, finely mortised ecosystem. Not only does the lowly barnacle do a lovely fan dance, she says, it distributes its larvae by the billions exactly when young striped bass are seeking food that size. "That integration," A.J. says, "that symphony of the water is what intrigues me."

A.J. stands for Alice Jane, and to know her is to know about integration. She has woven together a life that has artfully mingled two passionate marriages, seven children, a raftload of grandkids and an accomplished career that has harmoniously blended her fascination with science and her love of art. Stylish and pretty, her big blue eyes framed in a gamine face, she will not hesitate to grub in the mud to fish out a creature and study it in every stage of life, making her intricate renderings at every step along the way. And though her career began and thrived in the highly structured world of purely scientific illustration, she and her husband Robert Lippson—himself a well-respected marine scientist—have in the last two decades devoted themselves to bringing "that symphony of the water" to ordinary people. Their book *Life in the Chesapeake Bay*, now in its second edition, is standard fare on the shelves of high school students and ecologists, fishermen and Bay sailors. "It had always been in my mind to share with everyone the beauty and the wonder of the Bay," A.J. says. "We felt if people knew more about the diversity of species, it would make people even more interested in saving the Bay, so to speak."

Lucky for sea squirts and skilletfish that life has a way of changing the best laid plans. When she was in high school, A.J. knew she wanted to combine

science and art, so she set her sights on medical illustration. She was studying at Johns Hopkins Medical School when she met Romeo Mansueti, who was getting his doctorate in ecology, specializing in fishes. They married in 1954, and off they went to the Chesapeake Biological Laboratory in Solomons, Maryland, to study the early developmental stages of Bay fish. The lab in the early 1950s, she says, "was a very exciting place to be, at the leading edge of estuarine research. Then, you didn't even know what the young fish looked like, and here we were sampling them." Funded by the National Science Foundation, she and Mansueti worked together researching growth stages of white perch and chain pickerel, blueback herring and gizzard shad, among dozens of others. He wrote about them and she drew them in perfect technical detail. It was intriguing work and a happy, full life. And then Romeo died, suddenly at age forty, one week before the birth of their fourth child. "Fortunately, I had training," A.J. says in the understatement of a born survivor. She finished the work, juggling a newborn and three children under age eight, and in 1967 with Jerry D. Harty Jr., published *Development of Fishes of the Chesapeake Bay Region, An Atlas of Egg, Larval, and Juvenile Stages, Part I.* Notwithstanding her personal circumstances, it was a seminal work, her drawings detailing the growth of the tiniest larvae of dozens of species, hour by hour, day by day.

And when it was over, she was whipped. She packed her kids and her mother onto a Yugoslavian freighter and headed to Spain, to a small town near Barcelona. "I had to be by the sea," she says. "There's seawater in my system, I think." She enrolled her kids in an English-speaking school, visited the market every day and stumbled over her lousy Spanish, traveled to Germany for a month and went to Italy so her kids could visit their father's parents.

She came home when she was ready, and life intervened again, this time in the form of Bob Lippson, who had come to work at the lab while she was on sabbatical. He was studying crabs, and she started working with him on the water, digging in the mud. "He was dredging, and as he would bring the crabs up there would be wonderful, wonderful creatures that would come up, too, invertebrates and fish and everything. So I would go with him and we were so excited. With every haul we'd say, 'I wonder what's going to come up now?' " Eventually they married, joining her family of four with his of three.

A.J. continued her illustrating career, producing the award-winning *The Chesapeake Bay in Maryland, An Atlas of Natural Resources* and *Environmental Atlas of the Potomac Estuary*, a work that took six years to complete. By the early 1980s, the Bay's myriad health problems were coming front and center, and the Lippsons decided it was time to collaborate on their book *Life in the Chesapeake Bay.* The first edition, published in 1984, won instant, widespread praise. "This is the best written and best illustrated guide ever about a North American tidal estuary. It is the model for all future coastal nature guides," wrote the *Whole Earth Review.* The second edition, published in 1997, broadens to include flora and fauna further upland from the water's edge. "We never shed our scientific eye, but we were hoping we would become more like the old-time, quote-unquote naturalists," A.J. says.

At seventy years old, A.J. remains devoted to her calling and her family. Her home at the water's edge in Bozman, Maryland, is decorated with photos of her kids and grandkids and colorful, limber renditions of her art—watercolor washes of a cod and haddock, a quartet of sunfish in reds and oranges, a fleet

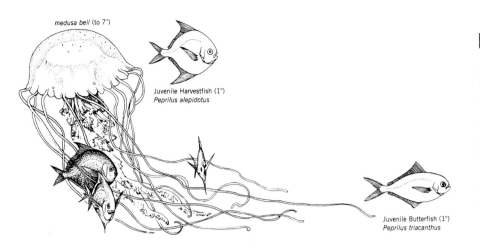

medusa bell (to 7")

Juvenile Harvestfish (1")
Peprilus alepidotus

Juvenile Butterfish (1")
Peprilus triacanthus

of mackerel, all shimmering blues and blacks. In a tiny loft upstairs, she and Bob continue to work side by side. "Watch the gnomes work on their book," reads a sign taped to a file cabinet at the entrance, "visiting hours 3 a.m. every fifth Sunday." Never one to be intellectually still, lately she's been studying art at Chesapeake College, turning her creative hand to painting in the style of the Dutch masters, her subjects born of the tidewater and the sea. And so she continues her singular celebration of life in the Chesapeake Bay. ■

Chesapeake Biological Laboratory

The Chesapeake Biological Laboratory, a part of the University of Maryland, is perched at the tip of Solomons Island, about sixty miles southeast of Washington, D.C. Offering spectacular views of the Bay, the Lab campus includes several historic buildings and a visitor center where visitors can learn about Bay fisheries, coastal issues, and ongoing research efforts to monitor and restore the Bay's health.

ISLAND HEART

From the water, as you approach the ferry dock at Ewell on Smith Island, the old workshop is inconspicuous. A small building constructed of wide boards and weathered gray, its swaybacked metal roof sags as if the sky itself is a burden. Like so much of this island's waterfront architecture, the workshop is simple, efficient and worked hard. Time, mud and countless tides have nibbled at the base of its walls, and sea grass tangles its edges. It is, to native islander Steve Evans, a treasure.

"Here's somethin', " Evans says as he scrambles over piles of stuff—baskets, ladders, crab pots, an old washboard—to reach a dim corner. He peers upward and points to the wall, where the dark scratch of a pencil's marks are still clear. They are blueprints of a sort, the lines and some measurements for a boat. Unassuming as the place may be, this is the workshop of Lawson Tyler, who until he died in 1965 was known far and wide for his tough, graceful little skiffs indigenous to this remote, remarkable island world in the middle of the Chesapeake. What would seem mere graffiti to an off-islander is an archive to Steve Evans, who in his own quietly tenacious way is working hard to hang on to these bits of Smith Island's past. "Stuff like this is interesting, I think," he says, digging through an old toolbox hung on one wall. "You never know what you'll find in here."

Evans is vice president of the Crisfeld and Smith Island Cultural Alliance, which operates a museum in Ewell just up from the ferry dock. He grew up on the island and still has family living there, though he moved off at age twenty-three. When he visits the island now, everyone calls him "Stevie" and he can't walk twenty feet without someone stopping him to jawbone for a minute or two. He builds houses and lives on the mainland in Crisfield, though lately he has become increasingly absorbed with the history of his hometown in one form or another. And this all really started, he says, with one of Lawson Tyler's skiffs.

In 1998, a group of people from Oxford, Maryland, built a Smith Island skiff and challenged the folks in Crisfield to a race. Their intention was to preserve a Bay boat design that was well on its way to extinction. Slender as a doll's slipper but stoutly seaworthy, these little boats were built initially for netting crabs in Tangier Sound's shallow grass beds. But Smith Islanders—who run boats like other people drive cars—naturally started racing them. "I'd always heard about the old speedboats—Smith Island speedboat is what they always called 'em," says Evans. "This type of boat will go through a sea two feet tall and you can sit in the bottom and you don't get pounded at all. It's amazing what they can do." The race in Crisfield went off smashingly, and the Smith Island Crab Netting Skiff Association was born. These days, the group has something like a dozen skiffs racing around the Eastern Shore all summer long.

One of them is Evans's, which he built about two years after that first race. "I wasn't real interested in it. Then I don't know, somethin' hit me and

I wanted to build one," he says. "I remember when I was little the boats laying in the marshes dying, like a lot of the boats do. It's like '57 Chevys; if I had all the '57 Chevys I tore up as a youngster I'd have it made." Built of cedar straight off the lines of the last known existing Lawson Tyler boat, Steve's *Island Queen* is a loving and historically accurate tribute to her forbears. He even painted the decks a bright pattern of teal and white, with starfishes, seahorses and crabs in alternating colors, because that's how he remembers the old skiffs being dolled up.

Island Queen got Steve Evans a lot of attention from the skiff association, enough that they made him president. Then the cultural alliance asked him to be on the board, and pretty soon, he was vice president. "That skiff gave me

more jobs," he laughs. But it's easy to see why. Quiet and slow-spoken, Steve is nevertheless persistent and patient in his efforts to snag a piece of history for the alliance's museum. One of its centerpieces is that last Tyler skiff, built sometime in the 1920s. Owned by the Calvert Marine Museum in Solomons, the skiff was in storage when Steve went to see it to get the lines for *Island Queen*. Then and there he began his efforts to convince the curators the skiff should return to its rightful home. After months of steady persuasion and a visit from the Solomons folks to ensure the skiff would be in a safe place, Evans got his wish. He helped load the skiff onto one of the island ferries and bring her finally to the center of the museum, where she remains.

Another gem in the alliance's collection is a crab scrape that islander Leon Marsh built for the museum before he died in 2001. *Beautiful Swimmers* author William Warner describes a Leon Marsh crab scrape thusly: "Its freeboard amidships was questionable, being not more than eighteen inches from the waterline to the rail … But in spite of its exaggerated beam it had a certain grace of line that unmistakably spoke of former days under sail." The scrape in the museum is lovely and perfect, but Evans has eyes for another—a tired, rough little boat tied up behind a crab shanty along a spindly catwalk of dock. Built by Lawrence Marsh, Leon's father, the boat has the scrape's plumb, fine bow fanning out into a broad, flat midships and stern. Evans believes she's the island's oldest boat still working and the last ex-sailing scrape. He climbs aboard and points out the rock-solid keel and the place where the centerboard was when sails drove the boat. "That's probably the reason she's still here," he says, rapping a knuckle on the boat's stout backbone. "That was some good wood back then. Hard to find that anymore."

Islanders have a term called "progging" (pronounced with a long "o"), and proggers are islanders who explore the marshy edges looking for who knows what—arrowheads, terrapin, muskrat, old bottles or ceramics. Or maybe old boats. On the way to Rhodes Point, where Steve grew up, he stops to lobby a waterman for a decrepit little craft, half-drowned in the stern with its bow resting on a bed of oyster shell. Evans has been pestering him gently for some time; he thinks he's getting close. The skiff was one of Leon Marsh's. Leon, Evans says, "was just unbelievable fittin' wood. His was just a different style. When he built 'em he would have varnish work on everything. He would even varnish the ribs and the coaming and the rails."

In the summer of 2001, Steve invited the skiff association's members to race the boats around the island to raise money so the alliance could buy Lawson Tyler's shop. Eight boats raised $7,000—enough to buy the shop and move it to a small lot next to the museum. As much as he can, Steve Evans will keep the old place intact, so you'll still walk on the paint-speckled wooden floors that smell of motor oil and sweat and salt marsh. You'll still be able to tug the line snaked through a sheave over the door that lifts a wooden "window" to invite a sea breeze. You'll still be able to stand in this old shop in all its well-worn, unaffected, imperfect glory, and learn something of the heart of Smith Island itself. ■

Smith Island Center

Reachable only by water, Smith Island consists mostly of an eight-mile long, four-mile wide swath of sand and salt marsh punctuated with tidal creeks and ponds. Although cattle once grazed over parts of the island, today its main economic activity is the harvesting of *Callinectes sapidus*, the world-renowned Chesapeake Bay blue crab. Three compact villages—Ewell, Rhodes Point, and Tylerton— share the island with the Martin National Wildlife Refuge. Smith Island Center in Ewell, operated by the Crisfield and Smith Island Cultural Alliance, is a compact museum with permanent exhibits on the waterman's life and island history, including the distinctive speech patterns that evolved in this isolated, windswept Bay outpost.

MAMA GIRL

Pigs are flying in Mama Girl's kitchen. A green one is leaping over the sink, its forelegs and wings folded tentatively and a look of alarm on its face, and a salmon-colored one is soaring under the stove hood, polka dots on its outstretched wings, all four legs flung outward, ears up, eyes and mouth wide open. Sheer joy is what this wonder pig is feeling. She probably didn't intend it—after all, a client simply called and asked her to make her a flying pig—but in a uncanny way, these two creations say a great deal about the woman who made them, the woman whose given name is Mary Onley but who is known to her friends, family and fans of her artwork as Mama Girl. With her feet firmly planted in the fields of Virginia's Eastern Shore and little more to launch her than a tenth-grade education, a fierce love for family and a commitment to the God she says directs her hands and her heart, Mama Girl has learned to soar with her unique folk art of newspaper, glue and paint.

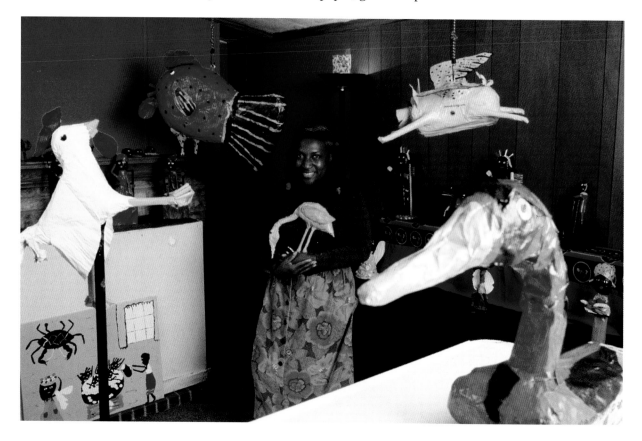

Everything about her is a surprise. Her studio in Painter, Virginia, is in a small house nested among an enclave of trailers and low buildings, hard by a road that branches off the main drag of Route 13 and snakes through piney woods and broad fields. This is rural country, this part of Virginia's Eastern Shore, where you sincerely respect the dog in the front yard and where the living is anything but easy for many of the people here. It is, without doubt, one of the last places you would expect to find an artist of Mama Girl's creativity and caliber, but you certainly can't miss her. A bright yellow sign out front glows like a sun, with "Mama Girl," a heart and an arrow painted in bold red pointing at the house. In the yard, ordinary resin chairs you get for seven bucks at the Wal-Mart are drenched in colors no manufacturer ever dreamed. Inside, color is everywhere, as if plainness is an evil to be banished. Ordinary wood cabinets are green, purple, pink, yellow, blue. Next to the kitchen table pushed against an orange wall, a skinny blue giraffe with yellow stripes stretches its head toward a blue tree dotted with small green leaves, and the faces of people are perched on the branches like smiling fruit. The kitchen table itself is transformed into a sky of blue trimmed with black vines and red flowers. Even an utterly pedestrian brown counter-top fridge is painted in waves of green and white. Where there once was a stove, newly finished pieces for an Adam and Eve scene dry beneath a heat lamp. In the room next door—what she calls her "trash room"—a table is littered with cups and cans of paint, a paint-spattered saucepan and brushes—all next to the water conditioner and the furnace.

And as for Mama Girl herself, though she is forty-eight years old—the mother of three grown children and now foster mother to ten-year-old twins—her face is smooth and unlined, her long hair pulled back into a braid that pours down her back. When she smiles, which is often, her cheeks dimple, and though her hands worked the fields for years, her fingers are elegant and unmarred. She and her artwork are like an exotic flower blooming in a moonscape, an oasis of rioting color in a barren desert. "I always liked to draw, but it didn't seem to amount to much," she says. "I would never get the colors right because I thought any color went together, and I still do, I'm not ashamed to tell you. Whatever come to me, I'll put it there."

She works in a deceptively simple medium—the newspaper, glue and paint of *papier-mâché*—but her creations seem to know few bounds. Pigs that fly. Dancing Chickens. Fish that are watermelons, watermelons that are fish. Gospel singers and field workers, Bible scenes and street scenes. All rendered with an unfettered freedom of form, shape and color. "It's pure. Nothing has gotten into her mind to mess up her vision," says Mary Miller, a textile designer who, with her husband, David Handschur, first met Mary Onley at a tiny show in Cape Charles, Virginia, in 1996. They bought "just an incredible cow" and offered to help her market and develop her business as mentors in the Eastern Shore Artisans Guild. "She doesn't have rules that somebody told her that this doesn't go with that. What comes into her spirit is what comes out of her hands. There's very little analysis going on there. It's pure. I can't think of a better adjective."

Mary Onley was born and raised here. Her mother was a factory and field worker, her father a minister and a mechanic. She has always loved being outside, and for twenty years she picked vegetables and was a crew leader in the fields. She always had a creative streak, too. "Ain't much I didn't try to make," she says. "I used to work with plaster, make mailboxes and things. I used to make clothes, dream up a design and get up and make it." Her days in the fields ended when ferocious allergies, which had affected her as a child, recurred in her late thirties. Her reactions to allergens were so fierce she would faint, and even going outside became a risky proposition. And so she turned to her hands again, and to prayer, asking God to show her what He wanted her to do. The answer came in newspaper, glue and paint. "I said, I have all this newspaper, I've been getting the newspaper seven days a week. I said if only I could make something with newspaper and glue. And I started praying, and right from the praying I turned out the first piece at three o'clock that morning. My husband got up out of the bed and said, 'When are you coming back to bed?' and I said, 'I'm finished now.' I said, 'Thank you Lord, I am going to bed.' And that was it!"

The first piece was an enormous bust of an African American woman, her hair cascading braids of paper, her gaze distant. The work was difficult, but she continued. Her husband, Donald, kept telling her she ought to get a real job, but her mother kept encouraging her. "She said, 'Keep on, it'll work.'" Eventually, the pieces piled up until one day in 1996, when Onley's daughter suggested she try selling some. She had heard about a little show in Cape Charles, paid the $10 entry fee and helped her mother cart the pieces thirty miles south to the Bayside town. Some of it sold, and two of the buyers were Mary Miller and David Handschur. When they offered to help Onley, at first she was unsure. A friend who knew Miller and Handshur told her, "Maybe they think you an artist." As she tells the story now, and whenever she uses the word "artist," she articulates it with emphasis, unconsciously holding it distinct from the rest of her colloquialisms. Brave enough to embrace the idea that what she was doing was art, she accepted Miller's and Hanschur's help, applied for and received a patent on her work, named her business after her childhood nickname, and began traveling to shows as far south as Georgia.

Onley's work has attracted collectors from Washington, D.C., to New York, Germany, Africa and Australia. It draws deeply from the rhythms and truths of the life she has known—a tall field worker whose hair blows back with the wind, a trio of gospel singers, a little boy playing with a bicycle, the Last Supper, Christ in the manger, Noah and his ark full of animals.

It has not been easy, and there have been times when she has doubted her decision to step completely out of her previous world. At one show, for instance, a man asked her why all of her human figures were African American. "I said, 'I'm sorry, sir, if I offend anybody, but that's all I know.' I said, 'I'm only doing what I see.' I came home and was feeling really depressed." And at some shows, people have ridiculed her art as juvenile, something a child could throw together. Onley has kept on, she says, because "the Spirit," as she calls God,

Ward Museum of Wildfowl Art

The Ward Museum of Wildfowl Art/J. Millard Tawes Historical Museum

The Eastern Shore has long been an inspiration for artists and artisans. An extensive collection of wildlife decoys, sculptures, and painting is on permanent display at the Ward Museum of Wildfowl Art in Salisbury, Maryland. Dedicated to the work and art of brother carvers Lem and Steve Ward, the museum also periodically hosts juried exhibitions of the work of contemporary Eastern Shore artists, with subjects ranging from Bay wildlife to evocative landscapes that capture the Eastern Shore's still-wild spirit—as well as its heritage as a haven for watermen and others with a passion for life juxtaposed between ocean and Bay.

To the south, in Crisfield, the J. Millard Tawes Historical Museum documents life on the lower Eastern Shore, beginning with the first encounters between Native Americans and European explorers in the 1600s. A working crab shanty brings to life the history—sometimes turbulent—of seafood harvesting in the region. A tour that embarks from the museum visits the Ward brothers' Crisfield home and workshop.

tells her she should, and when a collector asks her to create a flying pig, for example, as long as God tells her how to do it—right down to how much newspaper to use and what colors to mix—she will continue. "Everything I do is by faith and believing," she says. "It controls my whole life."

Not long ago, after becoming her most ardent supporter, Donald died from complications of a heart attack. Onley moved back home to care for her ailing stepfather and mother, and to guide her two foster children through school. Since her stepfather passed away, Mama Girl cares for her mother and children full-time, as well as maintaining a ministry from her house (she is an ordained minister in the Greater Harvest Community Church). Somehow amid these pressing priorities, her artwork continues to thrive, and collectors keep finding their way down the narrow, winding, backwoods road to her door. "I am surrounded by everything that I love," she says standing in the little kitchen-turned-studio, where all is bright color, and pigs can fly. "Everything." ■

Window on the Chesapeake

Of Birds and Butterflies

The wind is howling. Whipping down the Chesapeake, whistling past the concrete ships that serve as breakwaters at Kiptopeke State Park, it funnels up the road that leads from the fishing pier and beach and hisses through the grasses and loblolly pines. For the hawks, bald eagles and turkey vultures overhead, the wind is a glorious engine powering their effortless, soaring flight. For the members of the Coastal Virginia Wildlife Observatory, it's a pain in the neck. It's not even eleven in the morning, and they're already closing up the songbird banding station; the long rows of nets used to catch the birds are flopping around too wildly, and most of the birds are lying low anyway. The butterfly garden is pretty, but empty of fluttering visitors. And up at the hawk-watching platform, all this wind and cloudless sky make for a lot of stiff necks and strained eyes. Brian Taber's among them.

"We need clouds," he says. "Hard cold fronts concentrate the birds, and clouds help in seeing them. Gives contrast. They're 4,000 or 5,000 feet up today. Makes it hard to pull them out."

"Nice adult red-shouldered over here," calls a fellow hawk watcher, his eye glued to the Leica scope mounted at one end of the platform. Taber's binoculars, whose strap one suspects is surgically attached to his person somewhere near the nape of his neck, immediately assume the position to pierce the cloudless blue. Hang around birders for awhile and you'll quickly learn not to stand anywhere near the parabola defined by the length of their binocular strap—they could take your nose off with that thing as they snap their glasses to attention and, depending on the situation, either shout or golf-whisper something like, "Nice Cooper's above the trees!" or "My God! A vermilion flycatcher!"

Starke Jett photograph

Migrating thrush,
Kiptopeke Banding Station

You should expect this sort of behavior here at Kiptopeke State Park and nearby at the Eastern Shore of Virginia National Wildlife Refuge, for this is one of the best spots in the country to watch birds and butterflies on the move. Yellow-rumped warblers, Savannah sparrows, indigo buntings, brown thrashers, merlins, Cooper's hawks, sharp-shinned hawks, American kestrels and peregrine falcons—from August to December, millions of migrants heading south for the winter fly down the funnel that is the Delmarva Peninsula. When they get to the end—where Kiptopeke hugs the Bay side and the wildlife refuge the ocean side—many pull over and fuel up before undertaking the daunting fifteen-mile trek across the mouth of the Chesapeake Bay. Others backtrack north to try and find another crossing, and still others stay for the winter. Whatever their decision, it all makes for a smorgasbord of species for the researchers and volunteers of the Coastal Virginia Wildlife Observatory (CVWO). "Two weeks ago after a cold front, there were millions of birds here," Taber says. "It's the right place to be doing this kind of stuff. The numbers and diversity here rival anywhere."

This kind of stuff is research—counting, banding, recording, identifying as many bird species and, since 1998, monarch butterflies, as possible. (And yes, they do tag butterflies. Very, very carefully.) The Kiptopeke Banding Station, which opened in 1963 and operates August through November, has captured, examined and released more than 250,000 birds of 158 species. Kiptopeke Hawkwatch began in 1977 to identify and count raptors September through November. Since 1995, more migrant falcons have been documented here than at any other site in the United States, and the Hawkwatch averages 55,000 hawks of eighteen species annually. In 1998, the CVWO began a monarch butterfly migration study that has tagged more than 2,000 butterflies. And the spring migration program at the Eastern Shore of Virginia National Wildlife Refuge begun in 1999 has recorded more than 230 species and banded more than 3,000 birds. No small achievement for a non-profit organization that depends on passionate volunteers who routinely and willingly put in sunup to sundown days, and a few part-time research staff who do the same for a few intense months of work.

Window on the Chesapeake

....
143

Brian Taber is a founder and current president of the CVWO, which formed in 1994 as a way to merge the hawk and songbird research programs already underway, and to find money to ensure that the consolidated program would be able to hire professionals part time. While he is quick to shrug off his contributions and point to those of his cohorts and colleagues, his commitment is illustrative. A social work supervisor in his real job in Williamsburg, Virginia, Taber routinely travels the hours it takes to cross the Bay Bridge-Tunnel and head to Kiptopeke or the wildlife refuge for a weekend of birding. "There's always something that needs to be done," he says, whether it's tending the butterfly garden he established at Kiptopeke or stuffing the information boxes sprinkled throughout the park with CVWO brochures, writing grant proposals or helping count hawks, leading field trips during the annual birding festival or writing articles for the CVWO's magazine. Taber grew up "outdoorsy," and when a friend introduced him to birding years ago, he was hooked. "Once I got into it," he says, "I just wanted to learn more. It's a lifelong thing, and you'll never get to see everything." He has traveled from Costa Rica to Canada to study birds and their migratory patterns, and yet the southern tip of the Delmarva Peninsula never fails to amaze him in the numbers and variety of birds it attracts. "This is just a great outdoor lab," he says. "You come here at dawn and it'll be dark when we leave, and we say, where the heck did the day go?"

The organization's efforts to make bird research at Kiptopeke and the wildlife refuge more professional are succeeding. In 1995, the CVWO—with help from a grant from the Virginia Department of Environmental Quality—started hiring professional ornithologists to conduct the songbird and hawk banding and counting operations, with help from competent volunteers, during the peak months. They often come from around the country, broadening their own knowledge of hot birding areas, and their scientific contribution is immense, Taber says. The banding data goes to the U.S. Fish and Wildlife Service's banding lab, and the hawk count information goes to the Hawk Migration Association of North America. Researchers around the country and the world can then use the information. The more scientific the research, Taber says, the better the CVWO can advise state and federal officials on habitat management and other issues that affect birds, butterflies and raptors. For example, Taber notes, the loblolly pines near the hawk platform are thriving. That might seem like a good thing, but hardwoods provide far better shelter and food for birds than the pines. When the CVWO goes to the park managers to discuss thinning the pines and adding more hollies, sweet gums, oaks and maples, it will use the collected data to help make the case.

All of this has helped put the CVWO, Kiptopeke and the Eastern Shore of Virginia National Wildlife Refuge on the birding map, with stories appearing in the *New York Times, Washington Post* and *Birding,* the magazine of the American Birding Association. But while kudos, accolades and national recognition are always fun, they aren't what draws the volunteers who are braving neck cramps and eye strain today to spot hawks. Or vultures, in the case of Taber, who is eyeballing a group of about 180 of the birds circling above and looking, to the untrained eye, like nothing more than flecks of pepper against the blue sky. "I like vultures," he says, keeping his binoculars pointed straight up as he talks. "They're just so effortless. I've been seeing them for years and not really appreciating them. They have a well-developed sense of smell where most birds don't. I think I like them too because they're tropical—you go to the tropics and see them all over there." He keeps counting and watching and wondering, speculating on what the birds are up to and whether they'll cross the Bay today and head for North Carolina or wheel back to the north for some reason those of us who are landbound can only imagine. "Most of the people who come here just appreciate a lot of great birds," he says. "It's a spectacle I never get tired of." ■

Eastern Shore of Virginia National Wildlife Refuge

Just south of Cape Charles, at the tip of the Delmarva Peninsula, are Kiptopeke State Park and the 752-acre Eastern Shore of Virginia National Wildlife Refuge.

An amalgam of maritime forest and cultivated fields, grasslands, beach dunes, shrubby thickets, freshwater ponds, wetlands and marshes, the refuge provides a rich habitat for an amazing array of migratory and resident bird species. Shorebirds, game birds, and songbirds all live or make their way here, as do bald eagles and peregrine falcons. The fall migration period, mid-August through mid-November, is a particularly wonderful time for birding in the area. From September through November, birds of prey including osprey, hawks, and kestrels are banded here. Four-footed denizens of the refuge include red foxes, coyotes, and white-tailed deer.

Window on the Chesapeake

OLD TOWN RISING

It's evening, and though the autumn air is cool, somehow it still feels like summer walking the quiet streets of Cape Charles, Virginia. Maybe it's the trees that canopy the sidewalks—sycamores, maples, crepe myrtles and cedars that are hanging onto their leaves late this year. Maybe it's the sound of the Chesapeake Bay whooshing gently up the long, white beach that fringes the town's western edge like lace trim on a Sunday blouse. If it were summer, folks would be out in their front porch swings, or strolling their babies to the beach, or walking arm-in-arm, taking in the cool breath of evening and greeting their neighbors. But while the sun set an hour ago and the nighttime's chill has emptied the porches and sidewalks, the warmth of those quiet summer pleasures still seems to glow.

It'll grab you, a place like this, and you will care about what happens to it. Before you know it, you'll go along the streets picking up garbage, because garbage in a place this pretty is just plain shameful. You'll buy a wreck of an old building on the main drag whose porches had all blown off in various hurricanes, a building so decrepit it did not have a single living thing in it. Not even a rat. Then you might pour most of your money and all of your heart into restoring it, so that when people pass by, they stop and look twice. You'll spend countless hours talking with those people, and you'll hear what they have to say about this old blue-collar railroad town that has been cocooned for decades and only now is emerging, facing a world of tough questions about gentrification, poverty and wealth, environmental preservation and development, young working families and financially flush retirees, race and religion. And if you're not careful, you might end up working as town manager, a petite, blue-eyed, firecracker of a "come here" who can't hide the West Virginia in her voice as she faces down and sweet talks state agencies, multi-million-dollar developers and the fellow up the street who's had it up to here with the neighbor who won't keep his grass short enough. It happened to Cela Burge, anyway.

"I don't think it was an accident," she says. She found Cape Charles while vacationing with her husband John Burdiss and their kids. He wanted to go sailing. "That we came here on such a quirky thing, to go out in a sailboat. And I get here and there's a job that's perfect for me."

"We were really blessed when she came along," says six-term Mayor Alex Parry, who's lived in Cape Charles all his life. She didn't have any political experience, he says, but she had a background in public sector economic development. She also possessed "a go-get-em attitude, and the capability to handle many difficult situations that are going on in most communities, dealing with water, sewer, grants, people and the numerous state agencies you have to deal with."

Actually, that's the short list of what this town is dealing with. Founded in 1886, Cape Charles was the vision of William Scott, a Pennsylvania congressman and railroad baron, and Alexander Cassatt, who worked at the Pennsylvania Railroad's southernmost stop at the time, Pocomoke City, Maryland. Scott thought the railroad should come further south, but the northern bigwigs wouldn't bite. He did convince Cassatt, and the two of them formed the New York, Philadelphia and Norfolk Railroad. Scott headed south, picked the spot where he would end the railroad, bought 2,650 acres of land for $55,000, and set aside 136 acres just south of Cherrystone Creek that would become Cape Charles. He dredged a harbor on the southern side—making of the town a peninsula bounded by the harbor, creek, and Bay—and brought the railroad straight to the water's edge at the harbor, where barges still arrive to take on freight. It wasn't long before passenger ferries linked Cape Charles to Norfolk. Scott's tidy little town soon was bustling with families and workers, neat brick houses, stores, auto dealerships, theaters, restaurants.

But as Cela Burge will tell you, "communities have life cycles, just as surely as people do." And when the Great Depression hit Cape Charles, followed by World War II and a rocky economic landscape for the railroad, the pendulum swung. It has taken until now, really, for Cape Charles to revive, and like a boxer reeling from an eight-count, the rapidly changing town is a little shaky in the knees. Homes you could buy on a credit card eight years ago are now well into six digits. With the metropolitan Virginia Beach and Norfolk area just a $14 round-trip toll on the Chesapeake Bay Bridge-Tunnel and forty-five-minute drive away, "come heres" are beginning to outnumber "been heres." There's so much restoration of buildings and homes going on, scaffolding is a common lawn ornament. A developer who purchased most of what had been William Scott's extraordinary farm surrounding the town has built an eighteen-hole Arnold Palmer golf course on the town's south side, with another eighteen-hole Jack Nicklaus course to

follow. To accompany it, on the town's northern side the developer is building a community with lots ranging from $45,000 to $1.5 million, along with an upscale marina with space for boats up to sixty-five feet long. "We are seeing a lifestyle and a landscape changing before our eyes, and it's scary, especially for the people who've lived here a long time," says Burge. "But it's the challenge of every community to figure out how to re-invent itself. This is an opportunity for Cape Charles to mold and shape itself to give some of the people who have lived here some prosperity."

What hasn't changed, Burge says, is what drew her most in the first place: "Cape Charles is the new urbanist model. Other places are trying to artifi-cially recreate this. Cape Charles is the real thing—the whole idea that a community can be sustainable because it has these elements that allow people to live in a space that's comfortable, that you can live and work and recreate and socialize in one community." And it's small, just 1,200 people. "You really can know everybody who lives here," Burge notes. "You can really understand a problem and put a face on it." Those people represent every ethnic and religious background, as well as every economic class, and that diversity— all poured into one, compact, tree-lined, historic, waterfront pot—is what makes the town a spicy jambalaya of cultures, as well as problems.

You can see this mix from Cela and John's second-story front porch, which gazes out over the town's main street, Mason Avenue. Just a few doors down are a trendy new restaurant and an antiques shop. A performing arts center is housed in a restored 1940s film house, the Palace Theatre. Across the street is the supermarket and behind that is the rail yard, where old passenger cars rest on the rails and trains offloading onto barges are nearly daily visitors. Past the rail yard is the harbor, which just completed a $680,000 rebuild and has room for fifty-one visiting and resident yachts and workboats. And beyond that is the huge, erector-set landscape of Bayshore Concrete, a concrete fabrications company that helped build the Bridge-Tunnel. Some people, Burge says, dismiss the rail yard and Bayshore as warts on what could be an unblemished waterfront setting. But Burge—who, after all, is a coal miner's daughter—believes the town's hard-working past is vital to its sense of history and place, and thus to its future. "This is a working community," she says, "and it's been a working community historically."

What will happen to it in the coming years, Burge doesn't know. She only knows that she wants to be able to give her two cents—or maybe even ten. Maybe that means picking up trash on her way to work. Maybe that means watching the sun set over the Bay with John from their porch, giving thanks that he wanted to go sailing that day. Maybe that means convincing a developer to leave a big beach for locals, or making sure that a neighbor's grass gets cut. It's not an easy job mid-wifing a town through a rebirth, but it's a fulfilling one. "There is something," she says, "about when you're doing something that's good for people." ■

Cape Charles Historic District

With most of its original Victorian-era homes and commercial structures still standing—including the town's first building, then a barroom and now a pharmacy with a soda fountain—Cape Charles's historic district is the setting for some instant time travel. Events of various sorts relating to the special natural and cultural features of Eastern Shore life take place throughout the year, from historic garden tours in spring to annual events such as the summer's Eastern Shore Blue Crab Music Festival and a birding festival in October.

THE CHESAPEAKE BAY GATEWAYS NETWORK

This book features more than thirty sites in the Chesapeake Bay Gateways Network. These sites are listed below, along with basic contact information. Additional information on these and the dozens of other Gateways, including a map and guide, is available on the World Wide Web at www.baygateways.net.

Adkins Arboretum
12610 Eveland Rd.
Ridgely, MD 21660
410-634-2847

Calvert Marine Museum
14200 Solomons Island Rd.
Solomons, MD 20688
410-326-2042

Cape Charles Historic District
Cape Charles, VA 23310
757-331-3259

Chesapeake Bay Maritime Museum
Mill St., St. Michaels, MD 21663
410-745-2916

Chesapeake Biological Laboratory
UMCES, 1 Williams St.
Solomons, MD 20688, 410-326-7443

Chippokes Plantation State Park
695 Chippokes Park Rd.
Surry, VA 23883
757-294-3625

**Choptank &
Tuckahoe Rivers Water Trail**
10215 River Landing Rd.
Denton, MD 21629
410-241-8661

**Eastern Shore of Virginia
National Wildlife Refuge**
5003 Hallett Cir.
Cape Charles, VA, 23310
757-331-2760

**George Washington Birthplace
National Monument**
1732 Popes Creek Rd.
Washington Birthplace, VA 22333
804-224-1732

Gloucester Point Park
1255 Greate Rd.
Gloucester Point, VA 23062
804-693-2355

Havre De Grace Decoy Museum
215 Giles St.
Havre de Grace, MD 21078
410-939-3739

**Historic Annapolis
Gateway-City Dock**
Dock St.
Annapolis, MD 21401
410-280-0445

Historic London Town and Garden
839 Londontown Rd.
Edgewater, MD 21037
410-222-1919

Historic St. Mary's City
Off Route 5
St. Mary's City, MD 20686
1-800-762-1634

James Mills Scottish Factor Store
Virginia St., Urbanna, VA 23175
804-758-2613

**J. Millard Tawes Museum
& Ward Bros. Workshop**
3 Ninth St.
Crisfield, MD 21817
410-968-2501

Jamestown Island
Western Terminus,
Colonial Parkway,
Jamestown, VA 23081
757-898-2410

Jefferson Patterson Park and Museum
10515 Mackall Rd.
St. Leonard, MD 20685
410-586-8500

Kiptopeke State Park
3540 Kiptopeke Dr.
Cape Charles, VA 23310
757-331-2267

**Lightship Chesapeake
& 7 Foot Knoll Lighthouse**
Pier 3&5, Pratt St.
Baltimore, MD 21202
410-396-3453

Lower Susquehanna Water Trail
Call 717-299-8333 (PA – c/o Lancaster
County Planning Commission) or
410-457-2482 (MD – c/o Lower
Susquehanna Greenway, Inc.)

Mariners' Museum
100 Museum Dr.
Newport News, VA 23606
757-596-2222

Mathews Blueways Water Trail
PO Box 453
Mathews, VA 23109
804-725-4BAY

Pamunkey Indian Reservation
King William, VA 23086
804-843-4792

Point Lookout State Park
1175 Point Lookout Rd.
Scotland, MD 20687
301-872-5688

Potomac River Water Trail
Call 804-786-5046 (VA – c/o VA
Department of Conservation and
Recreation) or 410-260-8780 (MD –
c/o MD Greenways Commission)

Pride of Baltimore II
401 E. Pratt St., Suite 222
Baltimore, MD 21202
410-539-1151

Reedville Fishermen's Museum
504 Main St.
Reedville, VA 22539
804-453-6529

Smallwood State Park
2750 Sweden Point Rd.
Marbury, MD 20658
301-743-7613

Smith Island Center
12806 Caleb Jones Rd.
Ewell, MD 21824
410-425-3351

Sotterley Plantation
44300 Sotterley Lane
Hollywood, MD 20636
1-800-681-0850

Stratford Hall Plantation
Stratford, VA 22558
804-493-8038

Susquehanna River Trail
c/o Alliance for the Chesapeake Bay
600 N. 2nd St., Suite 300B
Harrisburg, PA 17101
717-737-8622

Tuckahoe State Park
13070 Crouse Mill Rd.
Queen Anne, MD 21657
410-820-1668

Ward Museum of Wildfowl Art
909 S. Schumaker Dr.
Salisbury, MD 21804
410-742-4988

Watermen's Museum
309 Water St.
Yorktown, VA 23690
757-887-2641

York River Water Trail
c/o Mattaponi & Pamunkey
Rivers Association
PO Box 197
Walkerton, VA 23177
804-769-0841

**Yorktown Visitor Center
and Battlefield**
Eastern Terminus, Colonial Parkway
Yorktown, VA 23690
757-898-2410

INDEX